SADO

*Lilies and the coastline
below Onogame*

SADO

JAPAN'S
ISLAND
in EXILE

Angus Waycott

Stone Bridge Press • *Berkeley, California*

Published by
Stone Bridge Press, P.O. Box 8208, Berkeley, CA 94707
TEL 510-524-8732 • sbp@netcom.com • www.stonebridge.com

Note: Throughout this book the names of premodern historical figures are, according to accepted convention, given family name first, while names of modern-day Japanese are in Western order, family name last.

Cover design by David Bullen.

Text design by Peter Goodman.

All photographs by the author.

Text and photographs copyright © 1996 by Angus Waycott.

All rights reserved.

No part of this book may be reproduced
without permission from the publisher.

Printed in the United States of America.

10   9   8   7   6   5   4   3   2   1

Library of Congress Cataloging-in-Publication Data

Waycott, Angus.
    Sado: Japan's island in exile / Angus Waycott.
      p.   cm.
    Includes bibliographical references.
    ISBN 1-880656-21-3
    1. Sado Island (Japan)—Description and travel.   I. Title.
DS894.59.N549S387   1996
915.2'1—dc20   96-15449
                                          CIP

*For Reiko, Bonnie, and Flora,
who often came too*

CONTENTS

A Word of Thanks   9

Map of Sado Island   10

DAY 1   A Minus Image   13

DAY 2   Sounding Echoes   41

DAY 3   Heart of Gold   69

DAY 4   Among the Exiles   92

DAY 5   Music through the Pines   113

DAY 6   Ship Horse Picture   140

DAY 7   Ball of Fire   166

DAY 8   Rafts Where Seagulls Crowd   190

Bibliography   207

A WORD
OF THANKS

I would like to thank Mr. Katsumi Kato, Mr. Tamotsu Isono, Ms. Izumi Mizushima, and Mr. Ryuji Sato for their friendship and their help with this project.

MAP OF
SADO ISLAND

Japan

SADO

Niigata

Tokyo

Osaka Kyoto

Sado Island

*Author's Route,
with principal places
mentioned in the text*

N

*Sai-no-Kawara
(cave)* · *Futatsugame*
Moura
Onogame · Washizaki
Kitaushima

*Ozaretaki
(waterfall)*
Iwayaguchi
· Seki
Kitakoura
*Shrine to
Mujina*
*Kurohime
Bridge*
Sembon
Uragawa

S O T O K A I F U

U C H I K A I F U

Hiranezaki
Tochu
*Mt. Kimpoku
(3,848 ft)*
ferry to Niigata
*Senkaku-wan
Quasinational Park*
Himezaki
(lighthouse)
Nojo
Himezu
RYOTSU
Suizu
Tassha
*Lake
Kamo*
AIKAWA
· *Kinzan*
Myosho-ji
Kasugamisaki
Niibo
(Tsukahara) · *Kompon-ji*
Noura
Takase
SAWADA
Chokuku-ji
MANO
Omedo
· *Toki-no-Sato
(museum)*
Hongyo-ji
Matsugasaki
Bentenmisaki
Shimokawamo
Oda
Osaki · *Togo-ji*
AKADOMARI
*Sobama
Beach*
ferry to Teradomari
Etsumi
*Sawasaki
(lighthouse)*
OGI · HAMOCHI
· *Shiawase Jizo*
Shukunegi
ferry to Naoetsu

0   miles   10

DAY I

A MINUS IMAGE

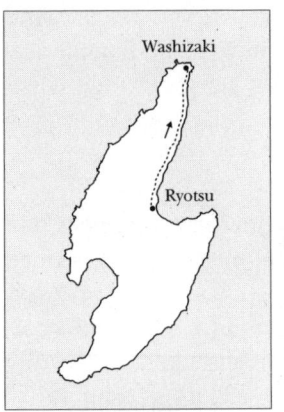

When I woke up, a crow was eating my last rice ball. It was my own fault, of course, for not having wrapped it more securely the night before. I didn't begrudge the crow a share, but the way he was eating it was all wrong. A few vigorous pecks had stuffed his own beak as full as it would go, but most of the rest of the rice ball had fallen in lumps onto the sand where, as far as I was concerned, they were beyond recovery.

Dawn had begun to lighten a cloudy sky. I sat up and stretched my arms. The crow flapped off. There was no one else on the strip of shingle beach, and the gray sea stretched unbroken to the horizon. I climbed out of my sleeping bag, put on my boots, and inspected the fire. It appeared to have burnt out: black-ended scraps of driftwood radiated from the middle like the spokes of a misshapen wheel. But when I held my palm over it, I could still feel some warmth. Collecting the dry twigs put aside the previous evening, I arranged them in a little pyramid and blew on the ashes until they burst into flame. Soon the

13

fire had recovered enough for me to boil a can of water and make some tea.

A few miles south along the coast lay Ryotsu, the main port of Sado Island, where I had landed the afternoon before. From the deck of the arriving ferry, my strip of beach would already have been visible: in fact there is nowhere else from which so much of the island's coast can be seen all at once. O-Sado, "Great Sado," the northern half of the island, looms ahead and to starboard, its blue and purple mountains rising steeply to a rugged ridge some 3,000 feet above the shore. To port is Ko-Sado, "Little Sado," the southern half, where the mountains are less forbidding and the coastline more benign: a patchwork of yellow-sand beaches, lumpy outcrops of volcanic rock, wooden houses clustered into hamlets around tiny bays, and green, wooded hills rising gently back to the horizon. And in between lies Kuninaka, the "Inside Country," the flat, alluvial plain that links Sado's two mountainous halves. Kuninaka is where the biggest settlements are, the most prosperous businesses, the widest roads, the best farms, the broadest rice fields, the most historic temples.

After the bustle and activity of the mainland, Ryotsu harbor in the afternoon seemed almost unnaturally quiet. A small truck buzzed by on the quayside road. Two women sat on a low wall, talking to a policeman. A bus driver appeared round a corner folding a newspaper, stuffed it into his pocket, and swung himself up into his cab. Two small boys chased each other along the pavement. Otherwise, not a sound, nothing to suggest that this place was the principal port for an island with 80,000 inhabitants.

Behind the town is a large lake called Kamo-ko, most of which is used for raising oysters. The lake is linked to the sea by a short channel, first opened by gale-blown waves about a century ago and later slightly enlarged for the purpose (never realized) of creating an inland harbor. The two villages on either side of the channel, Ebisu and Minato, were unified in 1885 to create the single settlement of Ryotsu, "Double Port," which was then officially designated as the island's gateway to the rest of the

A Minus Image

country. It's a relaxed, indolent little town, with a long main street, arcaded on both sides, a busy quayside fish market, several shrines and temples, and a network of side streets and back alleys lined with cheerfully dilapidated wooden houses. Another time I would explore it, but not now. It was already four o'clock. A week's walking lay ahead, and I wanted to get started.

Shouldering my pack, I set off to find the coast road heading north. On the way, I passed a temple with a graveled garden and a large statue of Kobo Daishi, the eighth-century founder of Shingon ("True Teaching") Buddhism and one of Japan's most famous wandering priest-monks. The statue's copper had oxidized, softening the original color to a pale and streaky green. Kobo Daishi towered above me on his concrete plinth. He was wearing a wide, bowl-shaped hat and straw sandals and held a staff in his right hand. There was a box in front of him for offerings. I tossed a few coins into it, and they clattered as they fell inside. Then I put my hands together, bowed, and prayed for a successful journey.

There was no traffic on the road out of town. The houses on each side had front gardens planted with shrubs, flowers, and fig trees whose small fruits were just starting to swell. A few also contained ponds where red and yellow carp lolled and splashed, rolling backward and forward among the rocks in lazy figures of eight.

Beyond these last outposts the town atmosphere, such as it was, quickly melted away. The first hamlets I passed wore a mellow, ancient, weather-beaten countenance, quite different in color from villages on the mainland. No concrete had been used in building them: all was plain timber, bleached by the sun. The shrine gates were made of unpainted logs, some freshly repaired, others rotten and crumbling away. Without traffic lights, advertising posters, or neon signs, all the colors seemed suddenly to have returned to nature: the browns of soil, mud, wattle, dust, weathered cedar, wooden tubs, tree bark; the greens of wild grass, cabbages in tiny gardens, young rice shoots planted in ranks in the paddies, leaves, the tangled scrub on the mountainsides; sudden splashes of yellow, irises,

15

marigolds, and maize; and huge blues of sky and sea, flecked with the white of clouds and wave crests.

Above a row of cottages towered a stand of tall bamboo, the leafy tops waving softly in the breeze like huge feathers. A footpath wound up from the road into its deep shade. Beside the path lay some long, straight stems left behind by the cutters, perhaps that same day. From three to five inches in diameter, they had been taken down with a single clean, diagonal cut at the base but had not yet lost their fresh, cool, powder green hue. Close by was a small woodyard, with more bamboo poles, some green, some brown, sorted into heaps according to size. A little white pickup truck stood just off the road, and there was a strong smell of freshly cut cedar. From inside a long shed I could hear the tapping of a chisel and the low hum of an electric saw.

I stopped at a small temple behind some cherry trees. The roof had recently been repaired and was covered with shiny black tiles. At each end of its ridge stood a clay dolphin finished with the same black glaze, head downward and tail in the air, a charm against earthquakes, typhoons, and other disasters. I clapped my hands twice to call the attention of the deity within, made a brief bow, and then raised my eyes again. Peering up through the leaves of a tall old cherry, I could see a large brown kite perched on the roof, its head cocked slightly to one side as if puzzled as to where the clapping had come from. I stayed still, and after a few moments the kite gave up on the problem, opened its wings, and launched itself flapping into the sky.

Birds can be seen everywhere along the coast of Sado—plovers, wagtails, sandpipers, gulls, and more, but the two commonest species are the crows and these black-eared kites, or *tobi*. Easily recognized by their long tails, the kites like to live on hillsides near the sea, where they build large nests of branches and twigs in the high forks of pine trees. When they're not looking down on the world from some convenient perch they glide silently above it instead, maintaining speed with occasional slow beats of their great wings as they search for little mammals, scraps of fish, or carrion. This diet brings them into direct com-

A Minus Image

Farm with rice paddies

petition with the crows, and aerial dogfights are frequent. In fact any other diet would have the same effect, since the crows eat everything, including garbage. Unlike the kites, whose nuisance value is offset by their elegant looks and regal manner, the fierce and muscular crows are universally disliked for a whole string of negative qualities: their harsh croaking, funereal plumage, quarrelsome nature, and generally arrogant way of strutting about.

In ancient times, things were different. Crows were regarded with reverence. This idea originated in China, where the species symbolized filial piety because the young were seen to feed and care for their disabled elders. Today that reverence has disappeared, although the crows' ready adaptability still arouses curiosity, and even a grudging respect. In the cities they live as resilient, all-purpose scavengers, foraging for food in the early morning by tearing open garbage bags and scattering their contents across the streets. One bird in Tokyo, the subject of a TV documentary, had become a true urban neurotic: it built a nest out of colored coat hangers stolen from washing lines and spent a good part of each day sitting inside it, barking fiercely at people in the street below. All in all, the commentator reported, crows in modern Japan have "a minus image."

Sado, too, has a residual "minus image" among the people of Japan, although modern tourist companies are working hard

17

to dispel it. The main reason is that for a thousand years the island's remoteness, inaccessibility, and fearsome winter climate made it one of the government's favorite places for sending undesirable people into exile. Over the centuries, a steady stream of disaffected aristocrats, scheming politicians, and nonconformist priests—not to mention thieves, sex offenders, arsonists, hoodlums, and other ordinary criminals—arrived for visits that were always long and often permanent. To make matters worse, judicial custom denied the exiles the right to know the length of their sentences. Removed at a stroke from their homes and familiar surroundings, they had no choice but to assume the worst and start life again from the beginning. What they endured, both from material deprivation and the agony of not knowing if they would ever be allowed to leave, was deeply impressed into the folklore of the island and handed down in plays, songs, and stories. As a result, Sado has a reputation as a sort of spiritual ultima Thule, frozen in heart as well as in fact. To the collective Japanese mind it stands for cold, melancholy, loneliness, separation, hopelessness, and despair. Not ideal, by the sound of it, for a walking tour. More like a recipe for chronic depression. Except that islands, by virtue of their isolation, preserve a whole range of natural and social conditions long after they have disappeared on the mainland, where development is more rapid. So that behind Sado's "minus image" might be more than one intriguing window on long-ago Japan.

I had only come a few miles from Ryotsu, but the sun was already going down on the other side of the mountains. Here on the east-facing coast, all was in shadow. Suddenly I was assailed by a gust of the sweet, heavy scent of clover: a large clump was growing on an embankment above the sea, and a few fat bumblebees, buzzing contentedly, were still gorging themselves on the nectar. At the foot of the embankment, the narrow beach was rough and littered with pebbles, none smaller than an orange, none larger than a melon. The sea was almost still. Tiny wavelets rose and rolled over on the stones with a chattering hiss right at the edge of the shore.

An old woman on her way home from the fields rounded

A Minus Image

the corner in front of me, trundling a barrow laden with vegetables. She wore *mompe* (work trousers), a pink-flowered smock, an ancient woolen jerkin, and short rubber boots. On her head was a shallow, circular straw hat secured by a white cotton cloth whose ends were neatly knotted beneath her chin. Seeing me, she stopped and set down the handles of the barrow.

"Where are you going?" she wanted to know.

"I'm walking up that way," I answered, gesturing ahead, "toward Washizaki."

"To Washizaki?" she exclaimed. "That's a long way. You won't get there tonight."

"No," I said, "I'll camp on the way."

"Camp?" she said. "Camp where?"

I looked around. "Maybe right here," I told her.

She glanced down at the beach, then back at me.

"Camping . . . ," she said thoughtfully. "What will you eat?"

"I've brought some food with me. I'll be fine."

She considered the idea for a moment, then smiled. This was obviously another of those foreigners who didn't know how to do things the normal way. People who wanted to camp on Sado came in the summer, when it was hot, not in spring. They didn't stay on shingle beaches either, but on properly appointed campsites. She looked into my face, still smiling. "Would you like something from here?" she asked, gesturing at the barrow.

There were some long white daikon radishes, a few cabbages, and several onions. An onion would go well with the noodles I had brought.

"That's very kind. Your onions look excellent." I picked one from the barrow. "How much would I owe you for this one?"

The old woman declined the idea of payment with a dismissive wave. "But later on," she said, "won't you be cold?"

"I'll keep the fire going after I've finished cooking."

That made sense. She nodded in silence. We had covered everything.

"Well, take care," she said. And with that she picked up her barrow and continued slowly down the road. But later,

19

SADO: JAPAN'S ISLAND IN EXILE

when dusk had fallen and it was almost dark, she reappeared carrying two rice balls wrapped up in a sheet of newspaper. "My husband said you must be hungry," she said with a smile. I thanked her, and before turning in, ate one of the warm, moist rice balls while sitting by the fire. The other one I saved for breakfast.

* * *

I left the remains of the second rice ball on the sand where the crow had dropped them. As soon as I had gone, it would be back to finish them off. In the meantime, it was killing time a little way along the beach, pacing up and down while it waited for me to go. Well, let it wait. I drank my tea slowly, watching the dawn sky lighten, and then tipped what was left of the water over the fire. After that I covered the place with stones and, to obliterate any trace of my having been there, did the same with the small patch of sand I had cleared to sleep on. Not that camping on the beach was forbidden, but "one who excels in traveling," says the *Tao Te Ching*, "leaves no wheel tracks."

Heaving my pack up onto my shoulders, I noted its weight with satisfaction. The first couple of hours of a walk are just long enough to tell you whether you are carrying too much or not. The last time I got it wrong, I was halfway up a mountain by the time the realization dawned. This time I had pared my requirements to the minimum. No tent, for one thing. It would be a mistake to come here without one in the height of summer, when the mosquitoes are at their worst. But May is a different story. Instead of a tent I had brought a large sheet of blue plastic, in which I could roll myself up, sleeping bag and all, like a long sausage. It was as rainproof as I would be likely to require.

Before setting off, I looked out across the sea toward the mainland, but there was nothing in sight. The distance is only forty miles or so, but it's quite usual not to be able to see from one side to the other. The wandering Zen monk and poet Santoka Taneda stopped on the opposite shore during the 1930s and wrote a haiku about it:

20

A Minus Image

Sitting here on this sand dune—
Today again
No sight of Sado.

Today, as in the past, Sado remains a place that people tend to pass by. They ponder its strange, bleak history while looking wistfully toward it from the opposite shore. Sometimes, like Santoka, they write poems about it. Even Basho wrote one. The inspiration must have come to him at night because it's about "the River of Heaven," the Japanese name for the Milky Way:

A wild sea—
And stretching across to Sado,
The River of Heaven.

It was time to get going. I looked around for a suitable stick to carry. All Japanese pilgrims and wanderers carried a staff, to lean on, to clear a path through undergrowth, and as a means of defense. I had also read that they banged it on the ground as they went so that snakes would hear it and stay out of their way. A few yards along the beach lay a bamboo pole that looked just right—an inch or so in diameter and six feet long, about as tall as me. I picked it up, tapped the ground with it a few times, and then clambered up the embankment onto the road. Clubbing the tarmac with a bit more energy than necessary, to get the feel of the stick, I set off toward Washizaki, the fishing port near the island's northern tip, about twenty miles away.

On the map, Sado is separated from the mainland by an unbroken stretch of clear blue sea, but in fact its two mountainous halves are peaks that belong to a long underwater range called the Sado Ridge. The island was formed by massive upheavals along this ridge that raised huge irregular blocks, marked on both sides by deep faults and tilted toward the west. Such upheavals, triggered by accumulations of pressure between tectonic plates in the earth's crust, exemplify Japan's general geological instability, its recurring pattern of violent earthquakes and volcanic eruptions.

Over the centuries these forces shaped Sado's topography, creating a jumbled landform of steep hills and mountains cut by shallow, swift-flowing streams opening into narrow valleys that broaden briefly where they meet the sea. Except for their grassy summits, the hills are clothed in thick scrub, bamboo, and deciduous trees like beech, oak, chestnut, maple, and cherry. Here and there can also be found irregular stands of conifers like red and black pine and *sugi*, or Japanese cedar. Once there were dense forests of hardwoods as well, but these were intensively logged for construction and shipbuilding, and for firewood, which used to be one of Sado's principal exports. A complex network of trails and footpaths, few of which appear on even the most detailed maps, still run like the threads of a web throughout the island; they mark the passage of woodcutters, charcoal burners, plant gatherers, hunters, traders, priests, and pilgrims.

For although Sado has always been poor and isolated, humans have lived there since earliest times. The sea yielded salt, fish, seaweeds, and crustaceans. The mountains provided edible plants, tubers, nuts, seeds, and wild fruits. Hunting was probably never more than marginal: Sado is too small and too distant from the mainland to have sustained much of an animal population, although there are badgers, rabbits, and other small mammals, plus a few pheasant and pigeons. In hard times, as elsewhere, the islanders would have had to fall back on snakes, snails, and lizards. But even before rice cultivation was introduced, a subsistence diet was there for the taking.

This is confirmed by prehistoric remains—tools, ax heads, ornaments, shards of pottery, grinding stones, beads, coins. Nearly all the finds have been made on the southern half of the island. Communities emerged later along the rugged northern shores. The secrets of the fertile central plain, obviously the most congenial area for settlement, are effectively beyond recovery. Flat as a carpet and already at sea level, the plain has subsided again and

A Minus Image

again over the centuries, gaining layer after layer of new topsoil washed down from the sides of the mountains.

The northern half of the island has always been the loneliest and least developed part. The shoreline from Ryotsu to the northern tip is called Uchikaifu, the "Inside Coast," because it faces toward the mainland. The other side, facing the Japan Sea, is Sotokaifu, the "Outside Coast." Between them is a twenty-mile-long ridge of mountains so steep and rugged and tangled that only a couple of roads cross it even today. Uchikaifu's only settlements are in places where rivers or streams have cut a way down to the sea, creating narrow valley mouths where natural terraces could be enlarged, leveled, and irrigated for growing rice and vegetables. Elsewhere, the mountainsides rise like fortress walls from narrow strips of beach, and the road winds obediently along at their feet, hardly deviating at all from the line of the shore.

That an adequate, well-paved road exists at all is due entirely to contemporary skills in engineering: twenty years ago much of it was a stony, unmade track with crazy, dangerous edges teetering above the sea, and twenty years before that there were sections where it didn't exist at all. Certain spots could only be passed at low tide, and even then only by scrambling over the wet rocks or running along the sand at the base of a cliff on the receding wave. Such problems discouraged travel among a population already little inclined to it, so that the far north was rarely visited. Poverty, a monotonous diet, and unsanitary living conditions were the norm. Every village, every family knew inbreeding and what came with it—bad eyesight, bad teeth, bad bones, stunted growth, and, often enough, stunted minds as well.

As in other remote parts of Japan, Sado's natural increase in population was offset by emigration. Many who heard tell of conditions elsewhere left to seek better lives on the mainland. But demographic records show that only a tiny proportion of the emigrants came from the most isolated parts of Sado. Between 1900 and 1950, as many as 40 percent of those who lived on the central plain packed up and took the boat, while in

23

the far north, where people had far more reason to want to leave, nineteen villagers out of twenty stayed where they were.

* * *

As I walked along, banging out a regular rhythm on the ground with the bamboo stick, I heard a car approaching from behind and moved into the verge to let it pass. Instead, it pulled up beside me, and the driver wound down the window. "Good morning!" he cried cheerily, in English. "I am Togashi, the Super Powerful Laughing Mushroom Farmer!"

I gaped at him for a moment in surprise. Mr. Togashi was a youngish man, perhaps in his early thirties. He had long, straggly black hair tucked up under a white knitted cap that made him look like a pixie. One of his front teeth was missing, and another was encased in gold. He beamed at me, as if meeting up with a long-lost friend.

"This my work house, look, here!" he went on, gesturing at a tumble-down shack beside the road in the shadow of a huge old cedar. "Please come in, we drink tea!"

He pulled off the road, jumped out of the truck, and gestured to me to follow him into the hut. At one end was a tiny room containing a table cluttered with magazines, bills, and papers, two broken chairs, a stool, and a gas ring connected by a red plastic tube to a cylinder of propane. He filled a battered aluminum saucepan with water from a tap above a small sink, placed it on the gas ring, and struck a match with a flourish.

I wanted to get this right. "You're a mushroom farmer?" I asked. "You grow laughing mushrooms?"

"Yes, yes, super powerful laughing mushroom," he replied with a broad smile. "Look, look here."

He rummaged through the papers on the table and handed me a paper sticker with his name, address, and telephone number on it. It was an advertisement for his business. The illustration was a drawing of the cap of a mushroom with female features crudely added—full red lips, pink blobs on the cheeks, and wide, round eyes with absurdly long eyelashes.

A Minus Image

"You eat my mushrooms, you dream, yes, make every girl pretty like this one!" he laughed.

I felt like I was dreaming already. Mushrooms, hallucinogenic or otherwise, thrive in Japan's damp climate, and there is indeed a species called *warai-dake,* or "laughing mushroom." But their consumption is illegal and certainly not suitable for commercial advertising. Sado was off the beaten track, but not that far off.

"Look, this my customer," continued Mr. Togashi, picking a slightly crumpled photograph out of the papers on the table. "This my customer in Tokyo."

The photo showed a woman in a sheer evening dress that clung to her curvaceous body and shimmered like the scales of a snake. She was standing in a dimly lit nightspot of some kind. Behind her, a few customers were sitting at a wooden bar, hunched over their whisky glasses. The woman had one hand resting casually on her hip. A lazy smile played around her mouth. She was every inch the girl who doesn't get taken home to meet mother.

Mr. Togashi handed me a cup of tea with an expression of amusement on his face. "It's good?" he asked. "You like my business? You want to work with me?"

"Well, it looks like a good business," I told him. "Where do you get the mushrooms from?"

"I grow," he answered, "grow mushrooms here. Come, I show you."

We put down our tea and I followed him out of the room and along a passage to a low door. Fixed to the wall was a panel with various knobs and temperature controls, which he checked and adjusted.

Behind the door was a dimly lit room about twenty feet square, entirely filled with shelves mounted on steel racks. A thermometer on the wall read ten degrees centigrade. Each shelf held several dozen plastic bags filled with a mixture of sawdust and rice husks, from which little brown buttony mushrooms were growing in clumps. They were *nameko,* a common, inexpensive species available in any supermarket.

25

SADO: JAPAN'S ISLAND IN EXILE

Fishing boats along
Uchikaifu

"These are the laughing mushrooms?" I asked.

"Yes, these! Ha ha! OK, laughing mushroom just joke. These *nameko*, we eat in soup, also with radish. Very delicious. You like?"

"Sure I like them. And you sell them in Tokyo? You send them down in a truck?"

"Yes, I send, sometimes I take . . . Tokyo, Yokohama, Shizuoka, Kanazawa, anyplace. This my business. Come on."

We went out of the room, closed the door, and returned to our tea.

"You come to Sado next time in . . .," he flipped one page back on his wall calendar, ". . . April. You come, we get *kogome*."

"You grow *kogome* too?" *Kogome* is a mountain plant, picked in spring as a young green shoot about the size of a little finger. You pay quite a lot for it in the cities when you can find it, which isn't often.

26

A Minus Image

"Not grow, find," said Mr. Togashi. He explained that he knew a good picking area in the mountains, a place where other people didn't go. It was his secret, he added, raising a finger to his lips. The season starts around the beginning of April. The first shoots are found at about 150 feet above sea level, after which you progress upward by 70 or 100 feet a day, depending on the weather, up to a maximum of about 2,000 feet. Mr. Togashi spent most of every April in pursuit of *kogome*, gathering twenty or thirty pounds in an average morning. Then he would carry his harvest home, eat lunch, and spend the afternoon washing, packing, labeling, and dispatching. He lived in a very old farmhouse with a thick thatched roof a little way down the road. It was a comfortable enough life, but . . . well, a little lonely. Restricted by having to remain at home and care for his aged mother—who else would do it?—he nevertheless wanted very much to get married and raise a family. But up to now, he hadn't been able to find a wife on Sado. The local girls wanted to move away, to live in towns and work as hairdressers, hotel receptionists, or shop assistants. The laughing mushroom talk, the stickers, the brochure, the letterhead, were simply to attract attention—attention that would expand his business, bring him new friends, introduce him to a potential bride. Could I perhaps suggest anything? We sat in the shack for an hour or so and talked about it. That is, he talked about it and I listened.

The problem was that entrepreneurial types like Mr. Togashi, although now becoming more common, were still the exception. Most of the people born along this coast either left to improve their prospects—that took care of nearly all the young women—or else resigned themselves to the traditional routine of village life, which meant long monotonous days of labor in the fields or at sea, leavened from time to time by seasonal festivals and ceremonies.

What happens when natural and economic conditions cause a remote community to stagnate in this way is very simple. Nothing happens. Evolution simply waits for a solution to come along by itself and break the deadlock. What solution would that be, here on the Uchikaifu coast? A few minutes after leaving Mr. Togashi's shack, I came upon the answer.

The next village, which was called Uragawa, showed evident signs of prosperity. There was a brand new post office, several old houses with shiny new roofs, several others in the process of being rebuilt, and a brand new harbor wall that reached out into the water and then curved back on itself, creating a safe, sheltered anchorage for forty or so fishing boats. The brash newness of everything was softened by a riot of early summer flowers; there were beds of marigolds, blazing orange, some cherry trees on which a few pink blossoms turning brown at the edges were still stubbornly hanging, azaleas coming into flower, buttercups, clover, and heavy bunches of wild purple wisteria hanging from the branches of their host trees. Beside the houses stood rows of *hagaki*, tall racks made of weathered pine logs lashed together with rope and used at harvest time for hanging up sheaves of newly cut rice to dry.

But the key to Uragawa's fortunes had nothing to do with nature or tradition. Its identity was revealed by a large, thick, beige-colored stain spreading out in the sea below, the sludge from a cement works. A dozen men in yellow hard hats were moving briskly around the site, filling and emptying molds for the production of concrete tetrapods.

The drive to modernize Sado, spearheaded by businessmen who want to expand the tourist trade and supported by local people who welcome the new jobs, has led to a boom in two industries: quarrying and concrete. Working in tandem, these are transforming the island, bringing wider, better roads, new harbors, and massive seawalls to even the remotest areas. Many sections of coast are now defended against erosion by long heaps of concrete tetrapods set up to absorb the force of the incoming waves. Most islanders approve of the changes: the aesthetic argument, which would preserve the landscape as it has always been, carries little weight. So eagerly has the gospel of concrete been adopted that the Uchikaifu coast is getting to be an aesthete's nightmare: more than half of it has already been "improved," and the pace of the improvements is continuing to increase.

A *Minus Image*

I stopped to buy a couple of rice balls at a small store in the middle of Uragawa, refilled my water bottle from a tap outside in the street, and then walked on a little way to Kurohime Bridge. If there is a god of concrete on Sado, this bridge is his best and newest shrine. It's about a hundred yards long and spans a small bay where the curving cliffs fall sheer to the water. The old road that was used before the bridge was built can still be seen. It passed through a low, narrow tunnel cut through the wall of the cliff, just wide enough for the passage of one small vehicle. Under incessant pounding from the sea, parts of the cliff have fallen away so that you can see into the remains of the tunnel; some sections were walled with timber and others, when the timber rotted or collapsed, with concrete struts. By contrast, Kurohime Bridge arches regally across the bay on massive concrete supports, turning the most difficult stretch of road on the whole coast into the easiest.

I sat on the bridge with my legs dangling over the side and munched a rice ball, recalling all I had heard about Japan's unique love affair with nature, the special affinity that enables the people to confront its benefits and drawbacks with the same unruffled composure. This is contrasted with the attitude of the less sensitive Westerner, nature's implacable opponent, dedicated to controlling, fighting, mastering, and enslaving it. The Japanese, it's said, never make that mistake. They appreciate their surroundings exactly as they are, live with them in a state of blissful, almost mystical harmony.

To walk up the Uchikaifu coast of Sado is to get a rather different picture. In Japan, like anywhere else, the enthusiasm for living in harmony with nature depends a lot on exactly which bit of nature you're obliged to live with. Urban Japanese, especially those whose homes include traditional rock gardens, patches of delicately colored moss, and attractive little waterfalls, tend to be keen proponents of the harmony-with-nature theory. Outside the cities, people are more practical. Island fishermen who can find no better shelter for their boats than dragging them up on a shingle beach, whose roads crumble without warning into the sea, whose homes are regularly flood-

29

ed out by spring snowmelt, don't have much to say about living in harmony with nature. They prefer to talk about concrete and the benefits it brings them. If you ask what they feel about the loss of aesthetic beauty, they shrug. It's a small price, they seem to imply, for such a vast improvement in comfort and security.

There is nothing unique about Sado in this respect. During the twentieth century, civil engineering may well have wrought more changes to the countryside in Japan than anywhere else in the world. There is hardly a river left in the country whose flow has not been diverted, channeled, and controlled by the installation of dams, concrete embankments, or both. Sheer cliffs by roadsides are routinely sprayed with a coat of wet cement and then covered with heavy wire netting, bolted into place, to prevent landslides. Operations designed to control nature—or, more precisely, to limit its capacity for causing damage—can be seen everywhere.

The reason is very simple. Japan's location and weather patterns have made it a land of dangerous instability. Volcanoes still cause devastation and death, typhoons still drag houses off mountainsides and smash them to matchwood, rain still bursts river banks and floods villages, minor earthquakes are still frequent, and the next really big one, as Kobe showed in 1995, is always just around the next corner. People who object to artificial interference with the landscape sometimes forget that effective civil engineering has a short history in Japan and that what went before it was enough to make anyone prize concrete above gold. What's interesting about the following sample of pre-engineering-era disasters is not only the extent of the damage caused, but also the brief time scale:

July 1888:	Bandai volcano erupts, 400 killed
Oct. 1891:	Earthquake, 10,000 killed, 300,000 homeless
Sept. 1892:	Typhoon on Tokushima, 300 killed
Oct. 1894:	Earthquake in Yamagata, 400 killed
July 1900:	Bandai erupts again, 200 killed

A Minus Image

Sept. 1902:   Earthquake in Yokohama, 200 killed
Oct. 1906:   Typhoon in Kyushu, 1,000 killed

Nowadays, such disasters are equally frequent, but meteorology, engineering, and more efficient, fire-resistant methods of building have dramatically reduced the degree of destruction. This is illustrated by a comparison with more recent earthquakes:

June 1964:   7.5 mag. quake off Niigata, 26 killed
May 1968:   7.9 mag. quake off Hokkaido, 52 killed
May 1974:   6.9 mag. quake off Izu Hanto, 30 killed
Jan. 1978:   7.0 mag. quake off Izu Oshima, 25
            killed
June 1978:   7.4 mag. quake off Miyagi Prefecture,
            28 killed
May 1983:   7.7 mag. quake off Akita Prefecture,
            104 killed
Jan. 1993:   7.8 mag. quake off Hokkaido, 1 killed
July 1993:   7.8 mag. quake off Hokkaido, 250
            killed

For other kinds of disaster, the effect has been the same. When a typhoon landed on southern Japan in September 1991, half a million households had their electricity cut off, but only six people died. A week later, another huge typhoon hit Tokyo and flooded 28,600 houses; this time the death toll was fifteen. The odds, at least, are improving. But then comes a massive quake like Kobe in January 1995, killing thousands, and upsets all the calculations again. Nature gets the last word.

In these circumstances, it would be surprising if the inhabitants of Japan had not developed a healthy respect for the power of nature, a respect quite possibly tinged with terror. Nor is it surprising that they claim a special experience of the earth and its forces and that they put a special value on staying in harmony with it, bending to its will, not fighting against it. The art of Japan does indeed suggest a close affinity with

31

nature, an acute sensitivity to its moods and changes. But necessity may be at work here quite as much as virtue. And it seems entirely right and reasonable that the villagers here on this lonely coast of Sado should welcome the improvements that concrete has brought. Because of it they live more safely, their houses have stronger foundations and don't get washed away, their boats are protected from even the fiercest storms. And if that's not mastering nature . . .

As if to emphasize the point, a serious landslide had blocked the road a little way beyond Kurohime Bridge. An untreated section of cliff—no cement coating, no wire netting—had collapsed from a point about 200 feet above the road and gouged out a basin some 150 feet wide. A chaos of boulders, soil, and broken tree trunks had tumbled down onto the road and over the edge on the seaward side. Several tetrapods lay smashed to pieces in the water below.

Repair work, of course, had begun right away. A narrow channel had been cut to allow one car at a time to pass through, and three small mechanical diggers perched at crazy angles were shifting the brown clay bucket by bucket to reshape the cliff-side. I asked one of the men how long it would take to finish the job, and he told me they expected to have the road fully repaired in about two months' time. "It's been a few years since we had one as bad as this," he added with a smile. "Not like the old days. Then, it used to happen all the time."

Beyond the landslide, not surprisingly, there was very little traffic. As I walked along in the early afternoon sunshine, it seemed as if I had the island all to myself. Occasionally the road avoided a dangerous section of cliff by disappearing into dark tunnels of rock, whose cracked walls and ceilings dripped with water. At the mouth of one of these tunnels I came upon the first snake of the day, its head neatly flattened by the wheel of a passing car. Only about a foot long, it was a young *aodaisho*, literally "Great Blue General"—the character *sho* is the same as the *sho* of *shogun* and signifies a military commander. The name also refers to the bluish slate-gray color of the adult snake's underbelly, but this was a youngster, earthy umber brown along

A Minus Image

the back and white as a fish on the underside. The reason for its failure to cross the road safely was easy to see: the stomach was swollen and distended by a recent meal, eaten but not yet digested.

* * *

A roadside sign announced that I was approaching a fishing port called Kitakoura. The road led down a hill past a complicated network of small paddy fields. These had been carefully terraced in descending levels so that they could all be irrigated by the same mountain stream: the water filled each little field in turn before being fed on through a section of pipe to the one below. Here and there scarecrows had been set up, their bamboo limbs clothed in brightly colored shirts and straw hats jammed onto their heads. Empty plastic carrier bags flapped noisily in the wind from the ends of their outstretched arms, and the features on their padded cloth faces were drawn with fierce, angry expressions.

Down by the harbor, the women of Kitakoura were hard at work. The task at hand was to fill up a pile of bags, each about the size of a large pillow and made of black, fiber-reinforced plastic, with coarse gravel, a heap of which had been tipped on the quayside from a dump truck. Two women held the top of a bag open while a third shoveled it full of gravel. Then they closed it by tying the top tightly with string. Each full bag was so heavy that it took all three of them to lift it, stagger a few yards, and heave it up onto the finished pile. They had already filled hundreds of these bags, which would be used as weights for the huge fixed nets offshore, and judging from the unused stack beside them, they still had several hundred to go.

In spite of this heavy labor, the group appeared to be extremely cheerful. There was a lot of chatter and frequent bursts of laughter. They were all dressed in the standard outfit worn by the women of Sado when working outdoors—short rubber boots, dark blue trousers, a pink or blue smock patterned with flowers, a knee-length apron, cloth or rubber gloves, and a straw bonnet whose brim extended forward

33

SADO: JAPAN'S ISLAND IN EXILE

around the face and was held in place by a long headscarf tied under the chin. They also had a small audience of fishermen who had knocked off for the day and were leaning against the pile of finished bags, smoking cigarettes and handing out advice. The sight of a foreigner passing through with a ruck-sack and a large stick promised an amusing diversion. They called me over for a chat. "What do you think of this, eh?" said one of them, gesturing at the work gang. "Japanese women are hard workers, don't you think?" They wanted to know if women in England did similar manual jobs, and were pleased when I said no. The women asked where I was going. "Why are you car-rying that stick?" said one. "Are you a pilgrim?"

I hesitated, unsure exactly what an affirmative answer might imply. The journey around Sado is not a formal pilgrim-age, as other routes are in Japan. There are two basic kinds. One is linear and follows a prescribed path between two speci-fied points. The other describes a roughly circular journey around a sacred area, which may be tens or even hundreds of square miles in extent and is filled with sites of special signifi-cance to the beliefs, legends, and practices of a given sect. Both kinds require the pilgrim to climb high into the mountains, fol-low forest and riverside trails, ford streams, sleep outdoors or in simple inns, eat local food everywhere, and call in at shrines and temples along the way to burn incense, bow, and pray.

"Well, not exactly a pilgrim," I answered. "The stick is to bang on the ground and frighten snakes away. Like this!" I struck the concrete quay a couple of times with Snake Frightener. They thought it was hilarious. "There aren't many snakes around here," laughed one woman. "Not here, but maybe in the moun-tains," said another. "Ah yes," said the first, more seriously. "Yes, maybe in the mountains. Be careful if you go in the mountains." She turned her head and looked away. The fishermen didn't want to talk about the mountains either. They wanted to tell me about the fishing. The season for the best tuna had just started, they said. Big ones, one hundred pounds, even two hundred pounds if they were lucky. A valuable bonus, to supplement their usual catch of *buri*, or yellowtail. "And how do you spend the day

34

A Minus Image

when the weather's too bad to go out in the boats?" I asked them. They looked a bit vague and mumbled something about repairing nets. "You mean you get to stay home and relax," I said, tipping my closed fist toward my mouth with the thumb extended in a gesture of drinking. They grinned sheepishly, and a few of the women chuckled in confirmation.

At the first bend in the road beyond the village I stopped and looked back at them. Some people say that Japan is the only country in the world where communism works successfully, and here at Kitakoura it was easy to see why. On the surface it was Bolshevik theory put perfectly into practice—everybody pulling together, cooperating in their work and their social life, believing in the same things, laboring cheerfully, not demanding a lot for themselves. Lenin should have come here. He might have discovered how such a system really evolves—by consent, not by compulsion. Instead, when he fled the Tsarist police, he went the other way, to Europe. If you look at photographs of him, the piercing eyes, the jutting beard, the index finger stabbing the air to emphasize a point, you can see that he meant what he said, that he was driven by genuine convictions. But you can also see the obstinate side to his character, the determination to be right about everything. He looks like a dogmatic schoolmaster, just the sort of man who *would* change world history by taking a train in the wrong direction.

The cliffs rose steeply from the roadside, thick with bushes and stunted trees, impenetrable except in a few places where tiny footpaths used by woodcutters and plant gatherers disappeared into the dark foliage. Mountains don't have to be high to evoke a sense of the unknown. Dark and steep is enough. And although few wild animals live in these mountains—no bears, no boar, no foxes—there are other things to be wary of.

I caught a glimpse of something red in the trees and ducked in behind them to take a look. It was a little shrine with an unpainted wooden mask hung outside on a nail. The mask had a fierce expression and a hooked beak, like a bird of prey. It was a mountain goblin, or *tengu*—not the long-nosed *tengu* whose representations can be seen all over Japan today, but its

35

ancient, birdlike, and much-feared predecessor, the rare *kara-su-tengu*. On a little shelf beneath it lay a dish with the well-pecked remains of a rice cake and a glass vase containing a single stem of white clover.

Like most other supernatural creatures, *tengu* evolved in the distant past for reasons that have long been forgotten. Some people think that they originated as personifications of the unseen, arbitrary forces of nature. Others declare that their implacable hostility to humans carries a distant echo of active resistance by some vanished aboriginal people, driven into remote mountain areas by the invaders who colonized Japan from Southeast Asia in the distant past. Still others suggest a foreign origin, pointing out that the word *tengu* is not Japanese, but a Japanized pronunciation of the Chinese characters *T'ien kou*, which denote an ancient class of demon, a sort of winged dog that swooped out of the sky in stormy weather to wreak damage and injury. But guerrillas or goblins, or both, must surely have been at large in the valleys and mountains of Japan long before the sixth century, when regular contacts with China began.

Wherever they came from, the *tengu* arrived equipped with a whole arsenal of magical powers. They could fly immense distances through the air, hurl rocks, uproot trees, and appear or disappear at will. Earthquakes, storms, and landslides were blamed on them. So were personal losses and accidents, lost shovels, broken pots, unexplained pains and afflictions. They took special delight in arson attacks on Buddhist temples and random acts of kidnapping, in which the victims would be carried through the air to secret hideouts and later abandoned in treetops or on temple roofs, too stupefied by their experiences to speak or move for days afterward. A favorite variation on this theme was to abduct priests or children and "entertain" them with feasts and dancing in splendid palaces: but the next day, the hosts and their palace would disappear, the delicious food would turn out to have been nothing but the dung of animals, and the precious gifts they had bestowed would be revealed as worthless rubbish. In this decep-

A Minus Image

Uchikaifu coastline

tion they are a bit like the rowdy and thuggish *kallikantzaroi* of Greece, which, "should they come upon a benighted traveller," wrote Patrick Leigh Fermor in his book *Mani*, "force him to join in their loutish gambolling, leaving him, at cockcrow, battered and groggy."

Descriptions of their appearance vary in the details, but rural folk knew them as having the body and limbs of a man, a mane of long shaggy hair, the face of a fierce predatory bird, wings of flesh, powerful claws, and a beak so strong it could "bite through swords." The mountains and forests they roamed had to be approached with caution and respect. Retribution for those who came to fell trees, hunt animals, or gather plants without making suitable offerings ranged unpredictably from minor annoyances like ax heads working loose or sandal thongs snapping to murderous attack and dismemberment on steep, inaccessible slopes or in jagged, rock-strewn ravines. Even up until modern times, charcoal makers and other mountain workers would start their day by placating the unseen *tengu* with gifts of rice cakes, prepared and set out a safe distance from human habitation. And as recently as 1860, official preparations for an excursion to Nikko by the shogun included posting notices in the surrounding mountains that peremptorily ordered the local "*tengu* and other demons" to immediately "remove elsewhere" for the duration.

In later times, the proliferation of wandering priests and *yamabushi* (mountain ascetics) provided a rich new source of opportunities for the *tengu*'s taste for trickery. Stories were told of traveling monks and nuns being abducted on the road, disoriented with intoxicating mushrooms, and corrupted by exposure to evil thoughts and obscene practices. Alternatively, the *tengu* themselves would take on the form of priests and roam among the people preaching false dogma and dispensing harmful advice. Distinguishing between real priests and *tengu* imitators became harder than ever; anyone who lived apart from conventional society was liable to come under suspicion. After all, when some strange, half-wild individual was glimpsed in the forest or came down from the mountains to the valleys and villages below, who could say whether he was a genuine hermit or a *tengu* in disguise? Yet to know the difference was important: one story, duplicated in several different areas, tells of a priest who was caught in the act of tossing pebbles onto peoples' roofs at night, hoping that they would ascribe the nuisance to *tengu* and pay him to perform an exorcism.

But even *tengu* must evolve with the times, and eventually tales began to be told of more benevolent specimens. This new breed helped humanity by revealing secret spells that would overcome the power of their evil cousins, by rendering assistance to people in need, and by teaching arts like swordsmanship or calligraphy. Some turned aside from their fire-raising habits and became instead the protectors of Buddhist temples, typically lodging in large cryptomeria trees or on rocky peaks in the vicinity. As popular fear declined, they began to be portrayed with long, ludicrous noses instead of flesh-tearing beaks, and people wearing long-nosed *tengu* masks became a common sight at Shinto festivals all over the country. Today, such masks can be bought in virtually every souvenir shop in Japan, while

A Minus Image

the old, bird-faced variety is much more rare. But belief in their existence, and shrines where they may be propitiated, linger on in many rural communities.

Dusk was beginning to fall as I rounded the last headland and came down the last hill into Washizaki. A few children were playing on the harbor wall, clambering around in the boats and jumping backward and forward across the mooring ropes. A man in a crisp white shirt, his day's work over, was locking up the post office with a large iron key. I asked him if he could recommend a place in town where I could stay. "You'll need one," he said with a smile. "Have you heard the weather forecast? There'll be rain tonight—maybe a big storm. No good for camping out. That's what you're doing isn't it—camping out? Now then, a place to stay . . . let me see." He thought it over for a moment and then shouted across to another man who was passing slowly by in a battered white pickup truck. "Nozami-san has started taking guests, hasn't he?" he said. "Would you mind dropping this foreigner off there on your way home?"

I heaved my pack onto the back of the truck, laid Snake Frightener beside it, and climbed into the cab. We drove past the harbor and out of the village a little way before coming to a halt in front of a shabby two-story building. The owner, a thin man with a bald head, dressed only in a set of long underwear, was sitting on the floor just inside the door. He was red in the face from drinking, and in a thoroughly welcoming mood. "Hello there," he said in a thick voice to the truck driver. "What's this?" I explained that I was looking for somewhere to stay. Did he have a room available? "A room? A room? Certainly we have a room," said the owner, waving his empty glass at me in a gesture of invitation. "Come in, please. We have lots of rooms. All empty—there's no one staying here at all. It's too early you see, the season hasn't started. Well, it has started. That's to say, it's starting now. Come in, come in." He hollered for his wife, who came running out of the kitchen wiping her hands on her apron. "Look, we have a guest," he told her. "He can speak Japanese. He's walked here, all the way from Ryotsu. He's an American. You are American, aren't you? Oh, English?

39

Well, that's all right. We get all sorts of foreigners here in the summer—English, American . . ." he paused, but couldn't think of any other varieties. "All sorts. And you can eat Japanese food, can't you? That's good. Because we don't have any food from your country. What is it you eat? Beef? That's right, beef. Ha ha! Beef!" He laughed uproariously at the very idea. "No beef here. Just fish. And rice. Go on then," he continued, addressing his wife, "take him upstairs, show him the room." With which he turned away from me, seized a large sake bottle by the neck, and poured himself out another glassful.

Instead of a single room, I was given two that adjoined— one to eat in, with a table and a TV set, and the other for sleeping. The owner's wife confirmed what the man at the post office had said. A major storm was brewing, and was expected to break before morning. I didn't care. I was stiff and tired and my feet hurt. But after a bath I felt a lot better, and better still when dinner arrived. There was a large salad, a whole crab, several kinds of pickled vegetables, a dish of octopus marinated with thin slices of cucumber, a dish of *ika somen* (raw squid cut into long, thin strips like translucent bootlaces), tender and delicious slices of raw yellowtail (an inevitable part of any meal in northern Sado), a whole grilled bream, and a wooden bucket full of steaming white rice. It occurred to me that I hadn't had a proper meal for more than twenty-four hours. After eating it I sat beside the open window and slowly finished a second bottle of beer. It was dark outside, but not quiet. On the other side of the road, the newly planted paddies were full of frogs, all croaking in unison. The volume had been increasing steadily ever since I arrived. There must have been several thousand of them, droning gutturally on and on and on without a break. On Sado, people say that the noise is like priests reciting the sutras. When I went to bed, it seemed more mechanical than that—like trying to go to sleep during a busy shift at the ball bearing factory. Not that it made any difference. Within a few minutes, I was gone.

DAY 2 | SOUNDING ECHOES

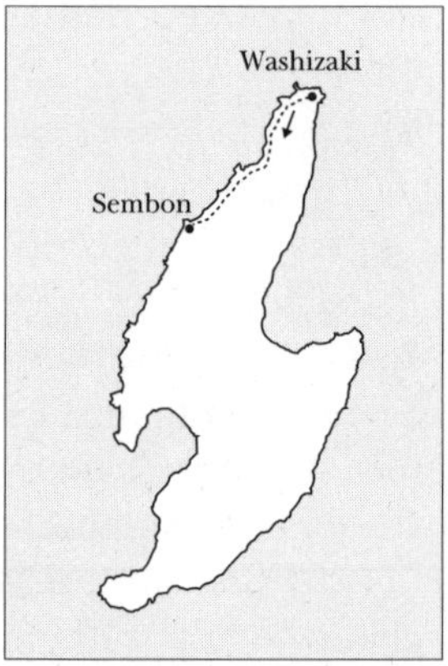

The Mogami Trough, the deep channel between Sado and the mainland, is a popular traveling route for *buri* (yellowtail), and catching them is the main occupation in Washizaki. In some parts of the world, *buri* grow as large as a man, but the commonest size around here is about two feet long and ten to fifteen pounds in weight. Their bodies are strong and streamlined, with short, bony fins and smooth, gunmetal-colored skin. Much of their time is spent on the move, which gives the impression that they are abundant everywhere: from early May to midsummer they migrate northward, close to the coast, and then return south in the autumn and winter, when their flavor is said to be at its best. These journeys are made in small, fast-moving shoals, usually at depths of between 70 and 220 feet—too deep for fishing by line or spear.

But up to about fifty years ago, line and spear was how most of the fishing on Sado was done, so catches were small and *buri* were only ever caught one at a time. The modern method is a lot more effective. A vertical wall of net is laid straight out to sea, at right angles to the shore, topped with glass or polystyrene floats the size of footballs, and weighted at the bottom with bags of stones like the ones I had seen the women at Kitakoura filling the day before. The *buri* feed along reefs or in rock holes near the shore, so sooner or later they come up against the net wall and find their way barred. Naturally they then turn toward the open sea and follow the line of the net, looking for a way round. But by the time they arrive at the end of it, they have already entered a complex, multilevel maze of traps from which there is no escape. All the fishermen have to do is go out every morning, winch in the nets that form the trap and haul the *buri* on board their boats. It's a lot easier than most forms of commercial fishing, and as long as the fish keep coming, it pays better too. There are a lot of new houses in Washizaki.

I emerged from the inn the next morning into a cool and cloudy dawn. It was five-thirty—the right time to go down to the harbor and watch the morning catch being gathered in. There was no sign of the storm I had been warned to expect. The ground was wet, so evidently some rain had fallen, but there was no wind and the clouds were pale gray, puffy, and light. The surface of the rice paddies was smooth and still: above them in the sky, a few kites wheeled slowly on outstretched wings, looking for something warm and bloody for breakfast. The frogs were well aware of this program, so their clamor of a few hours before had been replaced by a stony silence, broken only by a single nonconformist that was provoking the kites with occasional hoarse croaks. The kites didn't have it all their own way in the air, either. One, surprised in an act of thievery, suddenly appeared over the treetops and flew rapidly across the fields with two angry crows hot on its tail. Barking fiercely, they chased it long enough to make their point and then flapped haughtily down and perched together on a telegraph wire, glowering at the direction in which their quarry had disappeared.

Down at Washizaki's substantial new harbor—way too big

for the village fleet and therefore essentially another monument to the splendid possibilities of concrete—a few squid-fishing boats had come in during the last hour and were sorting out their catch. Some distance along the quay, far enough away to emphasize their owners' view that they were a different breed entirely, lay four battered work boats made of green-painted fiberglass, some sixty feet long and about ten feet wide. Each one had a small wheelhouse in the stern and a flat, open deck with a large hatch providing access to the hold. Their crews, dressed in heavy-duty waterproof suits and rubber boots, were taking on fuel, loading gear, checking their winches, or just standing around smoking cigarettes.

I asked if they would take me along, and they agreed willingly. We set off in a convoy, steering through the gap in the harbor wall and out into the open sea. A cool onshore wind was blowing, and the waves slapped the bottom of the boat with an irregular rhythm. Ten minutes later we arrived at the nets and took up positions that formed a rough square, with a hundred yards of sea between each boat. A young fisherman in the prow leaned over the side with a hook on the end of a long pole and recovered a black, greasy lead rope from the water. Someone else attached it to the winch, whose diesel engine sputtered a couple of times and then broke into a steady roar. All the fishermen then formed a line along the side of the boat facing the net and began to haul it on board, handful by enormous handful. Slowly the boats drew closer to each other as the great net was raised from the seabed. Soon the catch became visible—first the flying fish, jumping anxiously out of the water, then the *buri*, darting hither and thither like powerful silver torpedoes with their distinctive yellow-edged tails.

By the time the four boats came within touching distance of each other, the square of sea between them was churned to froth by thousands of panic-stricken fish. There were far too many for the net to be lifted completely clear of the water, so each boat now set up a simple block-and-tackle arrangement to which they fixed a scoop net, shaped like those that children use on the beach but much bigger, about four feet across, with a handle like a small tree trunk and netting like chain mail. Four men operated each one, lowering it into the main net, scooping up twenty or thirty *buri* and then swinging it round above the open hatch on the deck. Once it was maneuvered into position, they released a rope, and the bottom of the scoop fell open, depositing the fish into the hold. Using this method, it took nearly an hour to get the whole catch on board. The strays that fell on the deck—some sardines, some flying fish, a few squid, and a number of spiny, goggle-eyed porcupine fish— were thrown back into the sea. I picked up one of the flying fish and examined it as it lay gasping in my hand. It had a long, slim body, bulging round eyes close to the front of the head, and powerful pectoral fins, which also served as wings, emerging from the shoulders. Was it male or female? Now was their season for spawning, when the females swim close to the shore and lay their eggs in clutches that anchor themselves by means of sticky, trailing filaments to some handy stand of seaweed until hatching time. I studied the fish carefully, not knowing what to look for, then threw it back.

But for the *buri* there was no escape. As more and more of the net was drawn in, they found themselves with less and less space to move; packed together, they thrashed desperately at the water while waiting their turn to be heaved on board. Even more dramatic was the scene inside the boat's hold, which was half full of sea water and contained several large blocks of ice. Recognizing by the darkness and the smell of blood that this was the condemned cell, the *buri* responded to being dropped inside by going completely berserk. At first they barged up and down the hold in blind panic from one crunching collision to the next, until finally, too exhausted to continue the fight, they gave up and rolled over, lying still on their sides with staring eyes and blood trickling from their mouths as more new arrivals churned the reddening froth around them.

The task completed, the fishermen reset the empty net and turned for home. Between the four boats they reckoned they had caught about three thousand *buri*—a good haul, although they said the number was often higher in winter because the

Sounding Echoes

catch would build up during days when the weather didn't permit them to go out. Back at the harbor, they unloaded more huge blocks of ice from a truck and dropped them through the hatch into the packed hold. Then, having stowed a bottle of sake in the wheelhouse to enjoy on the way home, they set off to sell the catch to dealers from the mainland who would already be waiting for them at the market in Ryotsu.

I stood for a few minutes and watched them go, then turned away and climbed back up to the coast road. The sky was lightening and the sun was trying to come out. One strap on the pack had worked loose, and I stopped to adjust it beside an old, ivy-covered cherry tree with a deep cleft in its trunk a few feet off the ground. Suspended from the top of this cleft were thousands of large, fat ants all stuck together in a ball. They were clambering all over each other in a purposeful manner, as if convinced that they would finally find a way through the crowd to wherever they were going.

At the northernmost tip of Sado is a lighthouse, and a narrow road that follows the clifftop a little way before dropping down to a village called Moura. At a bend in the road at the top of the cliff was a graveyard for used cars; their owners had got rid of them by just pushing them over the edge into the undergrowth below. There were six Honda pickups that I could see, and one Subaru compact, all badly rusted and heavily overgrown, their corpses decoratively entwined with flowering convolvulus and pierced here and there by young saplings that looked like the shafts of spears.

The villagers of Moura were evidently less well off—or perhaps just less energetic—than their neighbors at Washizaki. There was an air of incipient dereliction, a cheerful disorder of frayed ropes, blackened old nets thrown casually across the seawall, piles of barnacle-encrusted floats, wooden boxes, barrels, a lead water tank, assorted bits of pipe, and other ironmongery lying around as though abandoned. The street was quiet, with a line of well-weathered wooden houses, some barely more than huts, on the landward side. A door opened among them and a toothless old woman with straggly gray hair hobbled out with a

45

bucket in her hand. She looked at me curiously and asked where I had come from, where I was going. When I told her, she nodded in a satisfied manner and then limped across the road and down toward the long, stony beach. Tourists use the beach in the summer, and their arrival has encouraged a few of the more enterprising villagers to abandon their former pursuits and go into the accommodation business instead. As old houses fall into disrepair, new ones are going up to provide bed and board to the visitors. Individual fishing is in decline, the business passing to well-organized cooperatives like Washizaki's, although small boats still go out from Moura every day to scour the offshore rocks and islets for shellfish and seaweed.

At the end of the village I took a path that followed the shoreline around the point. At least it used to be a path but had now been upgraded to a concrete track, just wide enough for a car or a small truck. The shore below it was littered with rubbish, not thrown out by the village but thrown back by the sea: the rusty door of an old refrigerator, some faded plastic bottles of sun oil, frayed scraps of rope, old shoes. Around and among them were growing the fleshy green leaves and cloudy purple flowers of wild vetch, which sunk its shallow roots into the pebbles and spread out in random patches like tattered rugs laid out in the sun to dry. The rockroses were also in flower, their deep pink blooms nodding gently on short, spiny stems, and stubby red pine trees clung to the rocks with scaly roots that gripped the ground like lizards' claws.

The path wound along the shore to Futatsugame ("Two Turtles"), a substantial offshore islet with two humps, joined to the land by a low-lying bar of pebbles and coarse gravel. Futatsugame is one of Sado's official beauty spots, pictured in all the tourist brochures, and no effort is spared to exploit it. The old hotel at the top of the cliff has been enlarged and modernized, and its grounds have been converted into an "autocamp," complete with hot-and-cold showers and flush toilets. Another campsite, for tents only, has been established in the pine woods just above the gravel bar. From here a flight of timber steps zigzags down to the sea. The bar effectively provides two beaches,

Sounding Echoes

one on each side, and in summer becomes crowded with families, beach umbrellas, flippers, and inflatable alligators. Sometimes storms cut the farther, narrower end of the gravel bar, making Futatsugame a true island; and then, days or weeks later, other storms put it back again.

There was a tent on the beach—the first sign so far that there were any outsiders on Sado apart from me—but the firmly tied flaps and the pile of empty beer cans outside told me that it was too early to stop and say hello. I walked softly around it and continued along the beachside path, which was narrower now and hemmed in by trees and undergrowth, so that I sometimes had to duck to avoid hitting my head on the low branches. A few wagtails strutted briskly along the rocky shore, batting the air with their long tails, and two kites launched themselves with slow, labored wing beats from the tops of two adjacent pines as I passed. But there were signs of human agency too: here and there I saw small heaps of stones piled carefully up on flat ledges of larger rocks and then some little clay figures, only two or three inches high, of Jizo, the patron deity of travelers. At first there were only one or two. Then more, groups of ten or a dozen, many overgrown by climbing plants and stained by growths of lichen.

Jizo is an all-purpose kind of deity who turns up in several different forms. As well as watching over travelers, his other manifestations include the Jizo of longevity (Enmei Jizo), the Jizo of pulling thorns (Togenuki Jizo), and the Jizo of stillborn, aborted, or miscarried children (Mizuko Jizo). Japan being a country where abortion is still a common form of birth control, he is very widely petitioned in this last-named capacity: people who have lost a child in any way often buy a small image of Jizo and dedicate it at a temple or some other holy place as a way of asking the god to guide the dead infant's soul safely across the Sanzu River, the symbolical border between this world and the paradise beyond. Another common form of the god is Migawari ("Scapegoat") Jizo, whose function is to take upon himself the earthly sufferings of those who petition him. When people pray to this Jizo to grant them a wish, and it is subse-

SADO: JAPAN'S ISLAND IN EXILE

Scattered Jizo figures near Sai-no-Kawara cave

quently fulfilled, they also make or buy a little statue of the god and leave it in some sacred place as a token of their gratitude.

As I continued along the path, I came upon more and more of these tiny figures set up on the rocks. There were hundreds of them. Finally the path crested a rise between two big boulders and came down to a tall cave in the cliff side whose walls were cut to make shelves and ledges, all crammed with Jizo figures. In the middle, on a plinth shaped like a lotus leaf, stood a larger statue of the boddhisattva with an infant in his arms and two others tugging at his robes in imploring attitudes. Around him were Jizo of every size and made of every material: stone, concrete, plastic, ceramic, even wood. Many were dressed in faded red hats and robes and some had tiny rosaries draped over their clasped hands. At their feet were offerings of coins and little dishes that had once contained food, along with hundreds of pathetically touching memorials to individual children—cans of orange juice or cola, a brand-new baseball, colored windmills on sticks, dolls, paper cranes threaded onto strings, well-known cartoon characters made of plastic. As I wandered round and examined them, a large crow flapped down and stood in the cave entrance behind me, croaking in mournful tones.

48

Sounding Echoes

The cave was called Sai-no-Kawara, which is also the name of the place on the shore of the Sanzu River where the dead must stop on their journey to the beyond and wait to be allowed to cross. Those who have done evil in this world must pile up stones as a penance until they are deemed fit to pass over the river and enter the afterworld. The spirits of children must also pile up stones, their "fault" being that while alive they did not have time to repay their parents for the gift of life. Out of his boundless compassion—and helped along, in the Buddhist tradition, by gifts and offerings from the living—Jizo eventually intercedes for them so that they too can cross the river.

All those Jizo, all those piles of stones, no sound but the waves curling and hissing in the rocks below—it was a strange, almost magical place, curiously beautiful, poignant, and touching, mystically sad. And yet . . . much as I profess respect for the religions of others, I couldn't feel right about Sai-no-Kawara. I tried. I sat and thought about it long and hard. But the end of every train of thought was the same: the theology of this thing sucks. This duty of children to "repay" their parents for the gift of life, as if it were some kind of transaction, smacks more of earthbound thinking and Confucian sociology than divine authority. More than once, people have explained to me why this view is wrong. They talk about eternal concepts beyond the individual, about cosmic continuity, about the wheel of life and death, about transmigration and reincarnation, about karma. In the abstract, it sounds good: too well-established to refute, too venerable to challenge. I don't really understand but that's all right, I'll buy it anyway. But here, seeing it in action, as it were, I realized that I didn't buy it. The main statue of Jizo inside the cave, with the children tugging at his robes, wore a faint smile of compassion on his lips, a smile that suddenly looked to me like the smirk of a complacent idiot. It made me feel like kicking him. Here are all these children waiting to cross the river! I wanted to shout at him. What are you waiting for? What else are you doing that's so important?

Beyond the cave there was a thick rope tied between two rocks and slung loosely across the path, a gateway to signify the boundary between this sacred place and the everyday world outside. It was a relief to pass under it and out into the village of Negai, where I restored my good humor with a cheerfully secular conversation about fish with a man who was arranging his tiny catch in a couple of boxes in the back of a truck. He didn't have a tooth in his mouth, which made his words almost impossible for me to understand, so while he named all his fish, described their characteristics and estimated their value—or perhaps told me about his wife's bad back—I looked behind him at an old bamboo frame set up for drying nets. Perched at one end of it was a bird I had never seen before, a bird with a splash of bright chestnut brown on its chest that made a dazzling contrast with the deep, slaty blue of its head and back. For a few moments it sat upright on its bamboo perch, loosely swinging its tail, and then suddenly flew off, low over the ground, and dived out of sight behind some rocks. I pointed it out to the toothless man and asked him what it was called in Japanese, but could only understand something that sounded like "Aaghphrk."

Up the hill from Negai was the headland called Onogame ("Great Turtle"), which crouches above the sea like a huge beast, its back and flanks clothed in coarse green grass that fades raggedly away to sheer cliffs the color of buffalo hide. The grassy area was temporarily transformed into a field of blazing yellow by the flowering of *kanzo* lilies, which grow wild all over Sado in late May and early June but nowhere so profusely as here. You don't so much walk through them as wade. The path to the summit of Onogame begins as a zigzag, as the slope is steeper than it looks, but straightens out beyond the point where the lilies finish and heads directly for the summit through a patch of dwarf oaks. From the top, marked by a stone lantern, there is a fine view back past Sai-no-Kawara to Futatsugame and another straight down the precipitous sides of the headland to some sharp rocks jutting out of the water like dragon's teeth. And away to the south stretches the long coast of Sotokaifu, the "Outside Coast."

The contrast with the "Inside Coast," where I had walked

Sounding Echoes

the day before, could hardly be more striking. The "Outside Coast" has no shelter at all: it faces northwest, straight toward Siberia, where most of Sado's weather comes from. Every winter, starting around early November, arctic winds scream across the Sea of Japan, sucking up moisture along the way and looking to dump it on the first bit of land they come to. The wind bites like a tiger and buffets like a bear, the snow whirls along horizontally in big flakes that stick to your clothes and blot you out, and the rain pours remorselessly down for days at a time. Clawed at by the sea, shaped and reshaped by earthquakes, battered by typhoons, Sotokaifu has been smashed and pulverized as though by a giant hammer. Everywhere there are bays and coves, pocket patches of shingle, boulders tumbled together, craggy offshore islets, tall stacks of fractured rock, shaded pools, and deep, narrow inlets. Few of these places are easy to get to and many are completely out of reach unless you approach from the sea. Others can only be reached by climbing, or lowering yourself on a rope.

With no industry to pollute it, the water along this part of the coast is always brilliantly clear. Beneath its surface, *awabi* (abalone) and *sazae* (a bitter-tasting shellfish commonly translated as "wreath shell" or "turbo shell" because of its spiral shape) cling to the rocks—both species, incidentally, may only be gathered by the islanders for whom they provide a living— and you can see shoals of yellow-and-black-striped angelfish, rainbow-colored wrasse, and perhaps a solitary octopus slowly pumping itself along beside you when you swim.

The worst enemy of the people who live along Sotokaifu is the bitter winter, evidenced by their custom of building houses low to the ground and end-on to the sea, in an attempt to mitigate the effect of the wind. Yet the climate is also a valuable friend, because although the summer is hot and sunny and richly productive, it is also short, too short to make tourist development worthwhile except in a few places that can be easily reached by road from the principal towns. No matter how much more wealth Japan may accumulate, no matter how much the tourist industry may expand, Sado's peculiar geogra-

51

SADO: JAPAN'S ISLAND IN EXILE

phy and weather patterns work to protect its natural features and traditional way of life.

With these satisfying thoughts in mind, I turned my face to the south and followed the wide swing of the road at the foot of Onogame. High in the cliffs, a waterfall was pouring out of a cleft in the rock and running down a steep channel to irrigate a network of paddy fields below. Automatic planting machines had already laid their rows of rice plants, but in order to get the maximum yield a few extra shoots were now being added by hand. An old woman in a wide-brimmed lampshade hat and thigh-length waders was slowly walking down each line and pressing a new plant in wherever she could find a space. She carried the shoots in a basket slung behind her, a broad basket with a narrow opening at the top to prevent the contents from spilling out when she bent down to the ground. We greeted each other, and she asked where I was going. "You've got a long road ahead of you," she said. "So have you," I answered, and she laughed.

There was an elderly soda-dispensing machine beside the road in Kitaushima village, but it looked as though I would need more than money to get a drink out of it. The labels of the different brands were faded to a mottled brown, and the money slot, change lever, and other visible components were crusted with salt and eaten away by rust. Nor was it aware that prices had gone up everywhere else in Japan. With more hope than confidence I dropped a 100-yen coin through the slot and pressed one of the buttons. A tinny, mechanical gurgle, like a voice crying out for a drop of oil, could be heard from inside, and then a cold can of plum juice rattled down a chute and fell into the collection slot with a clunk. I sat on the ground to drink it. An old lady with a white cloth round her face and shod in split-toed *jikatabi* workmen's boots plodded by, as if in slow motion, trundling a wheelbarrow full of firewood. There was obviously nothing to hurry for in Kitaushima. Nothing to do each day but get on with the tasks of life while the sun slowly wheeled its way from one end of the sky to the other.

Faced by a sheer wall of cliff at the end of the village, the

52

Sounding Echoes

road ran out of shoreline options and turned up into the hills instead. A short climb brought me to a hamlet surrounded by low, grassy slopes where the local farmers supplemented their inevitable rice paddying by raising a few head of dairy cattle. A rich odor of cowshit wafted through the air and bunches of freshly cut green grass were laid out across the road in neat rows to dry in the sun. An old woman in dark, Jizo-red clothes and a round straw hat was cutting fistfuls of the tall stalks from the roadside verge with a small, hand-held sickle. Another, having tended a mattress-size flowerbed in front of her vine-covered cottage, was carefully sweeping the uprooted weeds into a short-handled shovel. Water from a mountain stream gurgled down an old stone culvert into a patchwork of tiny fields whose earthen borders were crowded with buttercups.

One way or another, the land hereabouts seemed saturated with water—the still pools in the paddies, the invisible waterfalls splashing noisily among the rocks on the hillside, and droplets of moisture gleaming like gems in the folds of leaves. Flowering wisteria dangled from the branches of trees like grapes on a vine, and dragonflies darted around me in flashes of red, green, or electric blue, flying in short, arrow-straight lunges, changing direction, stopping and hovering, then darting off again. It seemed an odd way of flying. Was all that abrupt swerving to help them catch food on the wing, or were they trying to avoid predators? When they stopped to rest, it was always on top of a plant or a fence post, anywhere out in the open that left a clear flight path in all directions for rapid getaways. Not that their getaways were always successful, as the occasional crushed corpse in the road made clear. And, as I now saw, they also had to contend with human pursuers: a little way ahead of me, two small boys were busy trying to catch a couple to play with. The modus operandi was to wait for a likely prospect to settle somewhere, then approach it from behind, slowly and in silence. Then, very cautiously, the would-be captor stretched out a hand until his thumb and index finger were poised directly above and below one of the dragonfly's wings, without touching either; from this position he suddenly

SADO: JAPAN'S ISLAND IN EXILE

snapped them together, seizing the wing firmly between his fingertips but without damaging it. Then, while he held on tight to his vainly struggling prize, his pal carefully tied a length of cotton around its slender body. When they had each got one, they turned and strolled cheerfully back toward the village with their captives flying and buzzing on the end of the lines, like model airplanes or helium balloons, but far more interesting than either.

A sign beside the road announced that I was now approaching Kaifuohashi Bridge, an even more remarkable piece of engineering than Kurohime Bridge, which I had passed over the day before. Built of steel girders painted bright scarlet, it spans a deep, rocky, steep-sided gorge that winds far back into the mountains, too far for a mountain path to have been a viable way of getting to the other side before the bridge was built. The predecessor must have been some kind of ropeway, an unnerving thought in view of the hundred-yard distance from one side to the other and the two-hundred-foot drop to the boulder-strewn streambed below. On the seaward side of the bridge, the cliffs fell almost sheer to a long, narrow strip of shingle beach with rocks and caves at each end—inaccessible, as so often on Sado, except by boat.

Beyond the bridge, the sea could be seen through the clifftop pine trees in brilliant patches of azure and purple. The road passed through a short tunnel and then began to descend in long, tight zigzags to a village called Iwayaguchi, which is strung out along a wide, curving bay with a sandy beach. Halfway down I stopped for a rest beside Ozaretaki, Sado's most photogenic waterfall, where a mountain river gushes out over a lip of rock and tumbles for fifty feet in a curtain of foam into a clear, circular pool. The road makes a hairpin beside the falls, crossing on a narrow bridge with an old stone parapet. Far below, another solitary farmer was hand-planting rice in a group of paddies irrigated by the river.

At the bottom of the hill, the road straightens out to run alongside Iwayaguchi's beach—the widest, sandiest beach on the whole Sotokaifu coast. The word *kuchi* means "mouth" and

54

Sounding Echoes

the compound form, *guchi*, as in "Iwayaguchi," is commonly used to signify an entrance or an exit. The allusion here was to a tall, deep cave in the cliffside across the road from the beach. Yet another of the many miraculous constructions attributed to the roaming eighth-century wonder-worker Kobo Daishi, this cave was believed to be one end of a magical tunnel that extends almost the whole length of Sado to emerge close to the southern tip in a similar cave called Iwaya Dokutsu.

At the entrance to the cave was a circle of drystone wall that looked a bit like a Welsh sheep pen. There was also a statue of Kobo Daishi on a concrete plinth, several tablets of stone with the master's sayings inscribed on them, some mold-stained figures of Jizo, and two vases of dusty flowers. Inside, a few steps across the muddy floor brought me to the edge of a pool of water, whose extent was impossible to see in the darkness. But I could just make out the stalks of a few dead flowers set up as offerings in front of a low wooden platform. On this platform sat a doll, about eighteen inches high. Once it had been dressed as an elegant lady, in a fine kimono of red and gold, but after years in the cold and darkness, the clothes had all but rotted away. The body leaned unnaturally to one side, and the head lolled forward as if the neck was broken, the remains of the black hair dangling down as though from a corpse. It reminded me of the puppets used by shamans to summon spirits. Very likely it had been placed in the cave with some beneficent intention, but neglect had reduced it to something eerie and inexplicable, strangely appropriate to this dank, chilly place. I backed out of the cave and returned to the road, glad to get away.

But at the village of Seki, thirty minutes down the coast, something even stranger was awaiting me. Between a thick, twisted old cherry tree and a tall fir, a stony footpath led off the road toward a shrine. The dilapidated *torii* entrance gate was made from roughly sawn cedar branches now falling apart, crumbling at the edges into broken chips and fragments. Beyond it, the path turned a corner and disappeared into thick undergrowth. As I followed it, I found that it was spanned by a

55

succession of similar *torii,* around a dozen of them, all equally twisted and cracked with age, some with crosspieces dangling from broken joints, some leaning drunkenly to one side, some thickly entwined with ivy, and all so low that I had to duck my head to pass beneath them. On both sides of the winding path, half-hidden by shrubs and bushes, massive boulders were tumbled together in piles; occasional gaps yawning between them disclosed nothing but darkness beneath.

The tunnel of *torii* emerged into a small clearing completely surrounded by trees that obscured the daylight and threw murky shadows on the ground. There was a faintly sweet, woody smell, an aroma of decomposition, dead leaves, and fungus-covered logs mixed with the musty odor of animals.

Looking around, I could see that the place was—or had been—someone's home. Now in an advanced state of rot and decay, it presented a scene of almost medieval squalor. There was a derelict hut whose roof had partially fallen in, although a few old clay tiles were still attached by rusty nails to slimy green rafters. Through the broken windows I could see that the interior was a chaos of old garbage, plastic wrappers, discarded cans, and torn boxes. In front of the hut lay an open firepit and beside that a primitive shelter with a roof but no walls, erected over a stone trough that could be filled with well water for washing. In another dark hollow was a tiny wooden structure with air holes cut in the door, evidently a privy; two rotted boards on the floor had a rough hole cut in them above a deep cavity in the rock. The skeleton of an ancient bicycle, so badly rusted that it could certainly not have been ridden for twenty years, lay at an angle against the base of a tall tree. The wheel rims had almost completely disintegrated and the fragments of perished rubber that had once been the tires crumbled in my fingers like dust. Two or three hundred empty sake bottles lay in a large heap where they had evidently been tossed when their contents were consumed.

The centerpiece, as it were, of this pitiful hovel was a group of three or four large boulders. The top of one of them provided a low, flat ledge on which lay the remains of old offer-

Sounding Echoes

*Ozaretaki waterfall,
near Iwayaguchi*

ings—a few stained coins, a heap of pebbles, a plain glass jar, and some grimy little dishes. At the back of the ledge was the opening to a deep, dark hole whose floor, ten or fifteen feet below, was littered with more discarded rubbish and more sake bottles. A huge cedar branch, split off from its parent trunk, lay across the pathway almost parallel to the ground. I ducked under it, rounded a corner, and came face to face with a gray, rain-stained timber shrine. Along with the tunnel of *torii*, the presence of the shrine showed that this was indeed a place of worship. But of what kind? Why was everything so dilapidated? Elsewhere on Sado, as I had already seen, local people put a lot of effort into keeping their old shrines in good condition. They repair damaged woodwork, replace roof tiles blown away by storms, even add stone lanterns and other ornaments when they can afford them. What was different about this place? Why had it been allowed to fall to pieces? Hidden away at the end of its overgrown path, it had an air of secrecy, as if it lay outside conventional boundaries, deliberately set apart from the ordinary life of the local community.

I climbed the steps to the shrine and examined the objects attached to the front wall. Hanging from a nail was an old man's cane, with notches cut roughly into the handle and some characters in faded black ink inscribed on the shaft. Pinned beside it was a faded paper that looked like a list, though whether of names or appointments I couldn't tell. Plait-

57

ed cords of faded red and white silk ending in tassels dangled sadly from the eaves on either side of a thick, grubby white rope. Three moldering bags of some brocaded material were attached to the top like coconuts at the top of a ragged palm: when I shook the rope, they swayed slightly from side to side and emitted a soft, dry rattle.

My curiosity now thoroughly aroused, I made to open one of the sliding doors of the shrine. It moved easily to the side, revealing an inner door with two large panes of glass. Pressing my face up against it, I peered into the gloomy interior. What I saw gave me such a start that I nearly fell back down the shrine steps.

In the middle of the tatami floor was an old couple, staring back at the intruder with expressionless faces. They were quite still, as if posing for a photograph. The woman was standing, dressed in rough working clothes and holding a small hand towel as if she had suddenly stopped in the middle of some domestic chore. Even in the poor light I could see that she looked dirty, and her unbound hair was tangled and unkempt. Her eyes glittered; she seemed tense, wary, watching carefully to see what I would do next. The man was sitting upright in an old wicker chair at her elbow, dressed in a simple blue and white cotton kimono. His hands were folded together in his lap. Beside him on the floor was a glass-fronted box shaped like a little house, containing an ancient-looking drum with a short, stubby drumstick and a wand with white paper streamers folded in a zigzag pattern. Like his companion, the old man stared at me without moving. His brown eyes were close set and beady, his face was narrow, with pointed features, and his neat silver hair, combed smoothly backwards from a peak in the middle of his forehead, lay over his skull like a close-fitting cap.

Embarrassed by having almost forced an entry into what was apparently their home, I bowed quickly, muttered my excuses, and stumbled down the wooden steps back into the clearing. But the old couple's appearance, especially the man's, had solved the mystery. They were the resident guardians of a

Sounding Echoes

shrine to a *mujina,* the supernatural form of the *tanuki,* or Japanese badger. The tunnel of *torii* leading to the shrine represented the tunnel of a sett. The deep holes under the rocks were presumably present or former lairs, while the rock shelf on which offerings were set out was the *iwakura,* the place to which a spirit is summoned by rituals. The wand with paper streamers and the old drum were props used in the rites. So, no doubt, were the sake bottles.

"The tanuki," wrote Engelbert Kaempfer, a Dutch doctor who stayed in Japan for a while in the late seventeenth century, "is a very singular kind of Animal, of a brownish dark colour with a snout not unlike that of a Fox, and pretty small: it seems otherwise to be of the Wolf's kind." This inaccurate description accords well with the general confusion that seems always to have surrounded the mysterious *tanuki.*

The animal itself is real enough, though belonging to a species that is only found in Japan and a few places along the Amur River in Siberia. It is something like a raccoon, something like a badger, and is often called "raccoon dog" in English, for lack of a precise translation. In an otherwise light-colored face, the fur around the eyes and along the sides of the snout is dark brown, giving a raccoonlike appearance, but the *tanuki* is smaller and has a thinner, fuzzier tail. It eats anything and everything, berries, roots, snails, birds, fish, vegetables, and fruit and is nowadays increasingly seen in cities, where it comes to forage for food. It also raids farms and fields, showing plenty of ingenuity in evading capture: one farmer described to the local press how he had tried to protect his crop of Indian corn by covering the plants with netting and digging pits to trap the raiders. "I tried many tricks," he reported wistfully, "but they all failed."

No Japanese would be surprised by that, since the *tanuki* has long been known in legend and folklore as a deceiver with supernatural powers, as a trickster, and shapechanger. Sassy and impulsive, it is also endearingly simpleminded and often fails in its attempts to deceive people due to some foolish error, such as allowing its tail to stick out from an otherwise convincing disguise.

SADO: JAPAN'S ISLAND IN EXILE

Shape-changing animals are found in most countries—
Coyote in North America is probably the most famous—but in
Japan, such trickery is much more commonly associated with
the fox, whose exploits are recounted in tales and legends all
over the country. On Sado, however, it is the exclusive province
of the *mujina*. The reason is simple: there are no foxes on Sado.
A characteristic island story explains why.

> One day, a *mujina* called Danzaburo took a boat and
> crossed over the sea from Sado to the mainland to
> visit some of his old friends there. As he was walking
> along the road beside the coast, he met a fox.
>
> "Danzaburo," said the fox in a friendly voice,
> "you're just the fellow I was hoping to meet. Will you
> take me over to Sado with you, so that I can live
> there too? I hear it's a fine place."
>
> Danzaburo thought for a moment and then
> agreed. "All right," he said. "You can come back to
> Sado with me if you want to. But I may as well tell
> you now, you'd better turn out to be good at
> shapechanging. People on Sado are accustomed to a
> high level of skill and won't give you much of a wel-
> come if you can't deliver."
>
> "Hmm, I see," replied the fox. "Well, there
> shouldn't be any problem. Why don't I give you a
> demonstration of what I can do? Just name the trick.
> What would you like me to change into?"
>
> "Well, just before I met you I was about to turn
> myself into a human traveler," replied Danzaburo.
> "How about turning yourself into a pair of sandals
> for me to wear?"
>
> "Excellent idea," said the fox. And quick as a
> flash, he changed into a fine pair of sturdy wooden
> sandals.
>
> Danzaburo put on the sandals, made his way
> down onto the beach, and found a boat. He pushed
> it to the water's edge, jumped in, and put to sea.

60

Sounding Echoes

When he had gone some distance from shore, he
took the sandals off his feet and threw them over the
side into the water. The fox drowned—and ever
since then there have been no foxes on Sado.

Every *mujina* has an extensive repertoire of tricks, including the ability to impersonate real people, and is equipped with
an enormous scrotum that he drags about like a train, wraps
around himself like a kimono, or stretches out and beats on
like a drum. Particular individuals develop specialties of their
own, like stealing people's belongings from houses or temples,
conjuring up ghostly lights, or bursting into song from inside
bushes. One nasty-minded specimen makes a habit of lurking
along dark roadsides bent double, with his muzzle pushed
between his back legs to represent the female vulva, hoping to
lure some passing drunk into a mistake too horrible to contem-
plate. But although their shape-changing skills are sometimes
highly imaginative, they are usually employed in the service of
more modest ambitions. One Sado story tells of a man who
went to town and bought five fish. On the way home, he had to
cross a river, and while in midstream he suddenly noticed that
his load felt much lighter than before. He opened his bag and
found that the fish were no longer fish but had turned into five
ordinary sticks. Disgusted, he took them out and flung them in
the river. At that, of course, they turned back into fish, where-
upon they were caught and eaten by a *mujina* waiting a little
way downstream.

They also have the power of possession, which they may
exercise out of malice or to revenge some slight, such as disturbance to their lair or injury to their cubs. Others work directly
for a sorcerer, who wins their loyalty by feeding a pregnant
female and later receiving one of her cubs as a gift in return.
After this, the sorcerer can summon the cub at any time in
invisible form and use it to possess or harass an individual, usually at the behest of an enemy, who pays for the service. Or else
he can ask it questions about the future, or about other people's plans and secrets.

At the same time, *mujina* are also known to perform acts of kindness and are scrupulous about repaying favors. One story describes how a farmer was working in his field one day when he heard an anguished crying coming from down by the beach. A *mujina* had got its paw caught inside a shell, so the man helped it to get free. A few days later, the same man was out fishing in a little boat by himself when he suddenly heard a voice calling "Hey! Watch out for that octopus!" Looking round, he saw that a large octopus he had caught was clambering out of its container and trying to get back into the water. Thanks to the *mujina*'s shouted warning, he was able to recapture it.

Or again, there is the story of a *mujina* that disguised itself as a human and went to ask a midwife to come to its home and help with a difficult delivery. The midwife accompanied him to a splendid house she had never seen before and there supervised the birth, which was eventually concluded without mishap. But by the time her work was finished it had grown late, and the family in the big house invited her to have some dinner and then stay the night. When she awoke the next morning, she found herself out of doors under a big tree. The house had disappeared and the money she had been paid, which she had carefully stowed away in her purse, turned out to be only dried leaves. Realizing that she had been "over there," as it were, she carried the leaves home and dedicated them on the altar of her household shrine. A few years later, the village where she lived suffered a severe fire in which many houses were burnt down. But the midwife's, of course, was spared.

One striking feature of tales about *mujina,* especially to anyone whose idea of fairy stories involves drama and dragons and princesses being rescued from the jaws of unspeakable death, is their generally mundane story line and unexceptional details. The magic is of a very muted variety, lacking sensational climaxes and satisfying triumphs of good over evil. Instead, the tales record events and experiences that could happen to anyone. One reason may be that such stories *did* derive from real events, in which the strange or inexplicable element was ascribed to a *mujina* instead of to its more probable source,

Sounding Echoes

Onogame headland

the ascetic priest-hermit-wanderers known as *yamabushi*. *Yamabushi* were widespread in medieval Japan, including Sado, and practiced many of the skills—writing, healing, predicting the future, influencing the outcome of events—that *mujina* were supposed to possess. And since such skills were potential sources of money and power, unscrupulous *yamabushi* encouraged superstitious country folk to regard them with awe and hire them to solve their problems.

A further clue is contained in *mujina* names, which were often compounded with the names of sacred places such as rocks, waterfalls, or caves—Fuya ("Bamboo Grove") Mujina, for example, or Futatsuiwa ("Two Rocks") Mujina. Other names included suffixes (Tonchi-bo, Seichi-bo, Rei-in) normally applied to the names of priests. These compounds suggest a connection with Shinto worship in general and with *yamabushi* in particular, who were known to live in the wild, sleep in caves, and gain power by fasting, walking long distances, and standing under icy waterfalls. *Mujina* may therefore have played the role of mediums or familiars. But living so close for so many centuries, humans must have noticed long before the days of the

SADO: JAPAN'S ISLAND IN EXILE

yamabushi that their wild neighbor was weird, different, untamable; no good for food, or for work, or for companionship. Bold and cunning, it got into people's live and even their homes and then vanished, leaving mysteries no one could solve. What more natural source of tales and tricks could there be? It even spooked the language, spawning expressions like *furu-danuki*, meaning a crafty person, or *tanuki-neiri*, pretending to be asleep. Belief in its power was not something unseen but a matter of common experience. Worship at its shrines, too, was not deference to a superior but a simple enactment of rites designed to maintain the best available status quo: respect, food, and money from one side, restraint from the other.

The dilapidated shrine at Seki, dedicated to the worship of a *mujina* called Sabuto, was a vestigial relic of this once-popular cult. Evidently it was still in periodic use—the presence of the guardians and the pile of sake bottles proved that—and while not exactly secret, was hidden in the woods, away from public view, detached from mainstream religious practice. Although not yet completely obliterated, the trail into this strange cultural cul-de-sac is already badly overgrown and will soon, most likely, disappear forever.

* * *

Mujina apart, Seki has always been one of the gloomiest villages on Sado, and now that it's bypassed by a new stretch of road, it has lost even the feeble status conferred by having the public bus service pass through its main street. Instead, it has shrunk back to its former insignificance, huddled silently against the wooded mountains. There was no one in sight as I walked along the lane that wound between the houses, not even a dog or a cat. To one side of a low, rickety shack was a short flight of stone steps leading up to a path that disappeared into a clump of bamboo; the steps were so little used that they had become completely overgrown with clumps of daisies and patches of bright green moss. Irregular vegetable patches fronting onto narrow alleys, rusty wooden-handled farming tools leaning against plank-walled sheds, and piled-up bundles of straw and

Sounding Echoes

firewood all reinforced the impression of a hamlet barely changed since the Middle Ages. But signs of the twentieth century could be seen too, creeping over the village like a new strain of fungus. One battered old wooden house had been given an expensive face-lift with a new roof of bright red tiles, new double-glazed window frames, and a gleaming white circular dish for receiving satellite TV.

By walking through the middle of Seki I had missed the shortcut provided by the new main road, which passed under a chunky headland through a short, curving tunnel smoothly lined with concrete slabs and illuminated by glaring halogen lights. Sado's coast now has several of these airport-type tunnels, built to replace dubious sections of the old road that followed the very edge of the shore until forced to pass through short tunnels of their own. With their jagged, dripping walls, these tunnels were like galleries in an old mine: a modern safety inspector would close them without a second thought. But they weren't closed because of safety. They were simply too small for the huge buses that thunder up and down the island's roads in the summer tourist season.

The sort of vehicles that the islanders use could pass through these tunnels four abreast: when one drives through on its own, it looks like a child's toy puttering through an aircraft hanger. Apart from the charabancs, the only large-size traffic on the island is concrete mixer trucks. Nearly all the locals drive pickups or small sedans. Varieties of style and color are remarkably limited. Foreign car companies are fond of complaining that the Japanese market is rigged to keep them out, and so it is. But domestic shares are rigged as well. On Sado, for instance, Honda is preeminent: it looks to have the place stitched up like a sack of grain. There are also some Subarus and a few Toyotas, but hardly any Nissans, and I had walked all day without seeing a single Mazda. Osaka, by contrast, is Toyota country. Yokohama leans toward Nissan. That way, competition is restricted and profitability preserved. It's a crooked deal in the cities, but it makes sense in remote areas because the volume of demand is simply too low for all the

65

SADO: JAPAN'S ISLAND IN EXILE

manufacturers to maintain a presence, compete equally, and still make a profit. When the buyers are mostly low-income farmers and fishermen who all need basically the same thing, the most practical solution is to offer them one model in one color and pare costs to the bone. On Sado, the model is the Honda pickup and the color is white.

Tunnels have another use for the traveler on foot—shelter from the rain. It was just starting to spatter as I approached the tunnel outside a village called Koda. The sound of Snake Frightener clunking on the road disturbed a wild duck, which had been sitting in the long grass a few yards away beside a pebble-bedded stream. Straight away she flapped up into the air and flew around me in wide circles, emitting anxious honks. She had a nest down there and was trying to make it clear that she would feel a lot better if I went away. Taking the hint, I sprinted for the tunnel entrance just as the sky gave a rumble and rain from a black cloud began to thrash the tarmac.

I waited for ten minutes but the rain didn't stop. So I dragged on a plastic motorcycling suit, laid a short towel over my head and shoulders, jammed my cap back on my head, and set out again, looking like a cross between an Arab and an Albanian. Not that it mattered. No foreigner looks weirder than any other foreigner on Sado. See one, you've seen them all.

Koda was a nothing sort of village, just a shabby string of miserable-looking shanties with a little shop on the ground floor of the only concrete building. This was the headquarters of the local Nokyo, or Agricultural Cooperative, where the area's farmers brought their produce to be boxed up and shipped to town. The shop sold cans of fish and fruit juice, jumbo-size bottles of soy sauce, and various dried foods in plastic packets. I asked if they had any fresh fruit, but they didn't. Come to that, there were no fresh vegetables either.

The rain was blowing in squalls from the north, making patterns of dancing circles on the surface of the rice paddies and turning the soft, cool gray of the timber-walled houses to a wet, slimy brown. But there were flowers everywhere, tenacious climbing roses, clumps of oxeye daisies, and tall purple irises

Sounding Echoes

with three or four flowers to a stem. Each of these had three mauve-colored petals that curved upward and folded together at the top to form a little tent, and another three, darker in color, like protruding tongues, with dabs of yellow pollen on the end of their stamens. As I examined them, I heard voices call out a greeting from the other side of the road. Some young children were playing in the precincts of the village temple, sheltered from the rain by some tall cedars. They had been taking turns to ride a small, rusty bicycle, but the game had been interrupted because one of the stabilizer wheels had fallen off. "Can you fix it?" they asked. I looked around and found the retaining pin, which had come loose and dropped on the ground, and then replaced the wheel. "Are you a foreigner?" asked one. "Are you going camping?" said another. "What's camping?" asked the smallest.

Toward the end of the afternoon, I reached a place called Kogi. My feet were aching, and I was about ready to call it a day. The rain had stopped and the sky had cleared; all I wanted was to sit by the sea, drink beer, and then look around for a place to sleep. But Kogi didn't make it. It looked like a war zone. Another massive harbor was under construction, with rusty power shovels hard at work, bulldozer tracks all over the muddy ground, and huge piles of building materials lying silently under sodden tarpaulins. I half expected a destroyer to appear, or at least a couple of armed patrol boats, but as usual, all this building overkill was for the benefit of the local fishing industry. Tied up at the quay was a brand new squid catcher, apparently being made ready for its maiden voyage. Its paintwork was factory fresh, its varnished deck timbers gleamed a uniform golden yellow, and it bristled from bow to stern with the latest high-tech equipment—49 pairs of fat, elongated glass bulbs for the electric lamps, 8 radio masts, and 12 pairs of two-man reels, 6 along each side. But jutting out of the top of the wheelhouse, where I would have expected a flag on a pole, there was a long bamboo sapling with its leaves still attached and a couple of dozen folded twists of paper inscribed with prayers. Half a dozen men were sitting on the deck sharing a large bottle of

SADO: JAPAN'S ISLAND IN EXILE

sake. Either they were shy or else did not want to be interrupted: whichever it was, they all looked pointedly in other directions as I passed by.

I had better luck in Sembon, the next village down the coast. There was a scruffy campground with no one on it and a little roadside shop where I bought packaged noodles, an onion, and a few green peppers. I filled my water bottle from a tap in the yard outside, then went down onto the pebble beach and collected a pile of driftwood. It took two large cans of beer before the fire had stopped blazing and settled down enough to cook on. Dicing the vegetables into rough chunks, I gave them a minute or two in the water, heaved in the noodles, and then slurped up the mixture like a thirsty dog, gasping as it scalded the inside of my mouth.

Afterward I cleared a place by the fire to lay my sleeping bag and then wandered out onto a group of rocks at the end of the beach where there was a red *torii* gateway and a little shrine. The rock was badly faulted and trended sharply toward the sea at about forty-five degrees. The shrine was set up on a grassy ledge to one side of it; beyond were a few short sets of iron steps and walkways linking several huge boulders that enclosed a network of deep, sheltered pools. A man in long waders was crouching in one of the pools. He stood up when he heard my footsteps, and I saw that he was holding a dripping wire basket half filled with *sazae* shells. He gave me a few of the smaller ones, and I carried them back to the fire, arranged them points downward in the embers, tipped in a little soy sauce, and waited for them to start bubbling, which lifts off the hard protective cap and lets you get at the flesh inside. You pull them out with a toothpick or the point of a knife, and don't bother to examine them too closely because they look like twisty, three-inch sections of animal gut with some dark, sludgy, half-digested goo inside, which is pretty much exactly what they are. Just eat them hot and watch out for the grit. The flavor is bitter, but the flesh is tender and tastes of nothing but the sea.

68

DAY 3 | HEART
OF GOLD

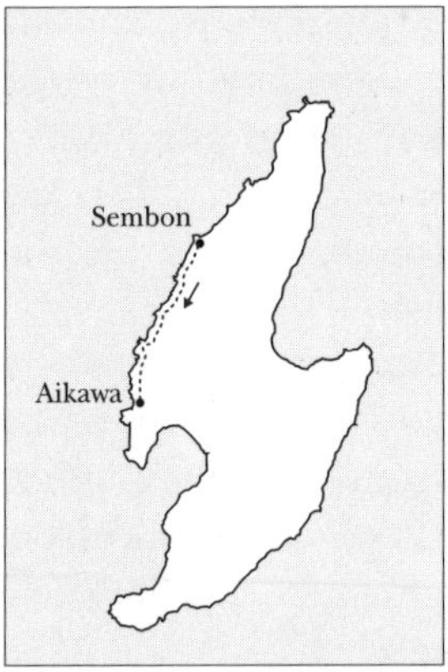

The sound of someone singing made me step off the road and down to a little shingle beach behind some big rocks. In the hour since I had set off I had seen no one at all, nothing but the dawn breaking over an empty world of stones and trees, wild yellow lilies coming into flower on the cliffsides, and the sea sloshing softly against the edge of the pebbly shore. Only the birds were busy, swooping and soaring across a wide blue sky peppered with blobs of white cloud that drifted slowly by like puffs of gunsmoke from some battle beyond the horizon.

A little old woman in dark trousers, a dark blue shirt, and a sleeveless woolen tunic was moving slowly along the beach collecting seaweed. In her left hand she held a bunch of what looked like long brown ribbons that glistened in the sunshine and in her right a thin bamboo pole tipped with a short sickle. Here and there she splashed out into the water and reached out with the pole to cut another of the fleshy plants and add it to her collection. As she worked, she repeated a strange, tune-

69

less little chant, the same few sounds over and over again, one of the old work songs of Sado.

When she had gathered enough, she hobbled over to a rock near where I was sitting and slipped on a pair of pink straw sandals with thongs of white rope. She didn't seem surprised to see me, nor alarmed by my foreign appearance. "Look at this," she said with a sigh, brandishing her bunch of seaweed. "It's no good any more, the *wakame*. Getting thin, and old. The season's coming to an end, you see. Soon it'll all be gone. And then we'll have to have *arame* instead—not nearly so tasty. And anyway, you need a boat. I won't be able to get it for myself."

We talked for a while, and she asked where I was going, where I had come from, the usual questions. "I'm a foreigner too," she said. "I wasn't born here. I come from Nagaoka, on the mainland." She was just a young girl when she left her family to come to Sado. She could remember them lined up by the door of her home to say goodbye, her mother and sisters weeping, wondering when they might see her again. It made a sad little picture. I changed the subject. "It must be cold here in winter," I said. "I suppose you get a lot of snow?"

"Snow? Here? Huh!" she snorted dismissively. "There's no snow here, nothing to speak of. The wind's cold, for sure, and strong, too. It blows the snow away, you see. Doesn't get much deeper than this." She held her hand out at knee height from the ground. "Now Nagaoka, that's a different story. That's real snow country. Why, the snow I remember when I was a child, it came right up to the top of the house." She gave a little cackle. "My father, he used to dig a tunnel for us, so we could get outside."

After we had talked for a while, I asked if I could take her photograph. "You don't want a picture of a weird-looking old woman like me," she said. But when I got the camera out, she looked pleased and struck a pose against a bit of seawall, her two wrinkled brown hands clutched around her bunch of *wakame* and her bamboo pole propped up behind her.

"Go on then," she said, when I had taken the picture. "Off you go now. That's your way, down that road to Hiranezaki.

Heart of Gold

That's where I live, but I'm not going back just yet. And next time you come, look me up. Bring your wife, too, and your family. Two daughters, you said? Yes, bring them along. Bring them to my house. We'll have miso soup, with *wakame* in it." And with that, she smiled and waved me away.

Hiranezaki is one of the "sights" of Sotokaifu and a popular place for tourists to stay because of its natural hot springs. Extending for several hundred yards, the shoreline consists of huge slabs of rock all tipped back at an angle of about thirty degrees to the sea, as if a long, straight, vertical wall of cliff had slowly toppled over backward without breaking up. This may be exactly what happened, perhaps due to some volcanic disturbance: the rock is pitted with tiny sharp stones like lava, and there are many deep, round sinkholes and blowholes where water was forced up to the surface.

At a bend in the road I could see the old hot spring bathhouse, now derelict. Its door and windows were all boarded up and the iron bars embedded in the rotting concrete had rusted through and bled great brown streaks down the sides of the dirty cream walls. On the other side of the road stood its replacement, a big new tourist hotel with a few tall, air-conditioned buses parked outside.

Around the corner, the road passed between two enormous rocks and onto a bridge that crossed a small bay. To the right lay the open sea, while the shoreward side was a steep cliff to which clung the hamlet of Tochu, its houses and shops and alleyways stacked up one level above the next, like an alpine village. A newly completed concrete jetty thrust out into the bay, and by the seawall a woman was pegging ribbons of green seaweed to a long string, just like hanging the washing out to dry. Below her in the water, a man in a grubby red baseball cap was drifting about in a rowboat half full of the same seaweed, poking thoughtfully at the water with a length of bamboo.

A little way ahead was the pride and joy of the Sotokaifu coast, a dazzling series of coves, inlets, and islets known collectively as Senkaku-wan, or Senkaku Bay. This is Sado's most famous beauty spot, and no tourist trip to the island is com-

71

plete without a couple of hours spent wandering its pathways, peering over the edges of its sheer cliffs, and poking about for gifts in its barnlike souvenir shop. Once again, it's a place where the coast is shattered to fragments by long-ago earthquakes, and the rock stacks that jut above the brilliant green and azure water are only the tops of mountain chunks jumbled chaotically together on the seabed. Tourists can go out in glass-bottomed boats, which, from the land, seem to follow an unnecessarily slow and tortuous route around the inlets; but on board, the passengers peering down into the long, rectangular viewing bay can appreciate the skill of their pilot. In some places, the rocks seem only inches below the boat and then they suddenly fall away, thirty feet, sixty feet down and more, down into the blue depths where shoals of *kurodai*, a kind of bream, swim straight ahead and all together, like dangerous bands of little black torpedoes intent on some unseen target.

To see what else there was in the way of sea life, I went inside the Senkaku-wan aquarium. Despite its importance as a tourist attraction, the place was endearingly shabby: the floor was in need of a good sweep and paint was flaking off the graying plaster walls. In the middle of the large room was a big tank with a lump of concrete inside, around which dozens of fish were constantly circling. There were a few small sharks arrowing through the water, several species of bream, and a solitary ray with the edges of its "wings" flapping gently like the hem of a skirt in the wind and a blank, expressionless little face peeping out from the underside of its head. Around the walls stood separate tanks containing striped angel fish, a few gloomy-looking squid, an octopus hiding inside a piece of plastic drainpipe, and several sea urchins slowly waving their long, black spines.

The sea theme continued at the souvenir shop, which was already filling up with the day's first arrivals. A dozen or so stalls set up outside were doing a brisk business in dried squid, seaweed, and jars of pickled fish. Among the souvenirs were some fine ceramic objects, including cups and teapots made of the smooth local red clay, but most of the rest were cheap and

Heart of Gold

tawdry: key rings, bead-encrusted handbags, colored hats, little dolls made of varnished bamboo, ballpoint pens and plastic lighters decorated with badly drawn nudes, packs of postcards, electric clocks, and gold-plated teaspoons. One considerate exception to the atmosphere of fierce commercialism was provided by a rack of fifty or so yellow plastic umbrellas: if tourists should arrive and get caught in the rain, they could borrow an umbrella without charge while they wandered round the complex. An island touch, I thought, when the shop could just as easily have had them on sale.

Senkaku-wan is a "quasinational park," a category of protected area that recognizes the established presence of homes and local industry but (theoretically) prevents further development or anything else that might damage the environment. But at Himezu, the next-door village, these restrictions were either suspended or else simply ignored. There was another massive new harbor, which meant a bigger squid-fishing fleet (and extra revenue all round) and a quayside scattered with piles of timber, gray roof tiles, and other construction materials. New houses were going up all over the place, replacing the decayed cedarwood shacks along the waterfront.

I was several hours too late for the daily excitement at Himezu, when the squid boats returned at dawn, their decks splattered with inky gore and their catches packed away in polystyrene boxes ready for shipment to market. But there were several long bamboo racks on which hundreds of the translucent, milky white creatures were laid out to dry in the sun, and a subsidiary fleet of smaller boats whose litter of crab traps and empty *sazae* shells showed that their fishing was done closer to the shore. Above them on the dock, weather-wrinkled villagers were patiently untangling their nets and refolding them in readiness for the next trip. Swallows flew around busily working on their nests, flitting hither and thither with twigs in their beaks and zipping past me at ankle level. When they fly low like that, said an old woman, looking up from her work with a resigned smile, it means that the rain is coming. And in fact as I set off to rejoin the main road above the village, the sun had

73

SADO: JAPAN'S ISLAND IN EXILE

Old woman with freshly gathered seaweed

already faded behind heavy banks of cloud rolling in from the sea, some of them ominously tinged with gray.

Ten minutes later I found myself standing on a high cliff above Tassha, the last village of any size before Aikawa, which was my destination for the day. A flight of stone steps led down from the road to a huddle of dark wooden houses at the base of a cliff that spread around a wide, curving bay with a beach of light shingle and coarse gravel. Two little boys, no more than five years old, were playing on the beach, dancing around a big bonfire that they had built out of driftwood.

The stone steps descended past a little cemetery where half the graves were decorated with bunches of big purple irises. A marmalade-colored cat observed me closely, without moving, as I went by. Down at the bottom, a narrow alley wound among the houses, and I came across a woman rinsing *wakame* in a blue plastic bowl, then tipping the salty water into a deep gutter covered with roughly worked slabs of stone. Other people too were busy outside their houses or working away in open-fronted sheds; they were sawing wood, making baskets, tinkering with boats, repairing winches, sharpening tools, stacking firewood. There were no shiny cars, no offices, no computers or neon signs or modern shops, no evidence of anything but traditional occupations, a kind of local self-sufficiency, as though people had nothing that came from a packet, but obtained what they needed from neighbors who had made it or sewn it or grown it or brought it back from the sea.

Heart of Gold

Even on Sado, such illusions rarely last much further than the next corner, and when I stepped out onto the beach I saw commercial reality reasserting itself in the form of three of Tassha's well-known "shark" boats, which lay moored together in a line beside a short jetty. These have nothing to do with fishing, but make up a small fleet of launches for carrying tourists along the rocky coast to look at the glories of Senkaku-wan from the sea. The cabin section of each one is an elaborate wooden superstructure, pointed at the front, with glaring eyes and a fierce toothy mouth painted on, rising in the middle to a tall, sharp dorsal fin on the roof and then sloping down at the back with another long fin on each side. From the outside, it looks as though the passengers are being carried along inside a big fairground shark. The blue one and the red one were empty, but a handful of tourists were quietly waiting in the green one for the next departure, while just at that moment the yellow one, returning from its first trip of the morning, rounded the headland at the other end of the bay. Behind the jetty there was a tourist center, with a car park, shops, and restaurants, so I bought a box lunch of rice and fish and pickles, plus a can of beer, and carried them down to eat on the beach.

* * *

The sky hung lower as I walked the last few miles along the cliffs to Aikawa, and a few preliminary drops of rain made dark spots on the sidewalk as I clumped round the last corner and entered the town. Wooden houses lined both sides of the road, interspersed with dingy shops selling such practical items as work clothes, paint, gardening tools, fishing nets, and parts for boat engines. Before reaching the town center, I turned away from the coast and took a road leading up toward the cloud-shrouded mountains that loomed above the town. It was a quiet, narrow lane that wound this way and that as it climbed, past an old school with a badly overgrown playground, past a yard containing a few rusty mechanical shovels, past some garden allotments planted with flowers and vegetables. Finally I

SADO: JAPAN'S ISLAND IN EXILE

left the last one behind and plodded on alone up a forbidding-looking valley with forests of beech, maple, and mountain cherry on both sides. By this time the sky was black and glowering, the air as thick and heavy as treacle. From somewhere in the hills came a rumble of thunder. I wondered if I could reach my goal before the storm broke. It would be a close thing. A half-rotted wooden sign nailed to a nearby tree warned that I still had a little way to go. "Kinzan," it said, "1.5 km."

Kinzan, or "Gold Mountain," is Sado's most famous landmark, and the mine from which it took its name—the biggest and most valuable ever found in Japan—redefined the island's place on the national map. From the time it was discovered in 1601 until it finally closed in 1989, work went on practically without interruption. On the backs of men and pack animals, the recovered ore was lugged down the narrow, rainy little valley into Aikawa for smelting and refining. The pure gold was then hammered out into sheets, and the sheets were cut up to make flat, oblong "coins" called *koban*. Packed in boxes, a thousand at a time, the *koban* were transported across the island to the southern port of Ogi and loaded onto special, vermilion-painted ships that took them to the mainland for transport overland to Edo. More than half the total yield in the mine's history was obtained during the Edo era, and the wealth it produced made a vital contribution to the stability and continuity of the shoguns' rule.

Mixed deposits of gold, silver, and copper, according to geologists, are often to be found in areas of "intense tertiary volcanic activity"—and in the case of Japan, that means pretty much every part of the country. Sado certainly had its share. By the twelfth century, and probably much earlier, the islanders already knew that there was gold in their rivers and streams. Small amounts were often recovered by panning.

The first serious attempt at mining took place in 1542, when a merchant from the mainland province of Echigo organized the exploitation of a vein of silver at a place called Tsurushi, east of Aikawa. But the discovery of Kinzan was on a different scale altogether. The apocryphal tale recounts how a

76

Heart of Gold

fisherman was rinsing his net in a stream one evening when his eye was suddenly caught by moonlight glinting on a nugget embedded in a rock. Following the stream back up into the hills, the man found other rocks with similar deposits, and eventually traced their source to a mountain called Doyu-no-Wareto. Today, the peak of this mountain is split by a deep "V," a formation explained in Sado's tourist literature as having been brought about by a mythical miner who, "in his feverish zeal for gold, drove a spike into the top of the mountain and split it in two!" This dramatic suggestion is not as fanciful as it sounds: the spot is an old open cut working of one of the main veins, probably among the first to be discovered.

When the news about Sado's mountain of gold got out, things started happening fast. The island's provincial status, which dated back to the eighth century, was summarily revised by Tokugawa Ieyasu, the ruling shogun, who immediately placed it under his direct control. Two years later he appointed a certain Okubo Nagayasu as *bugyo*, or commissioner, with instructions to organize and increase mining output, administer the island, and ensure security by maintaining strict surveillance over neighboring parts of Japan. Successive *bugyo* carried out these duties until 1867, assisted by a staff of civil servants and police.

At the same time, the gold rush was on. The population of Aikawa, until then a sleepy and insignificant fishing village, rose from a couple of hundred to about 120,000 in only ten years. Miners, carpenters, foundrymen, tool-makers, workers of all kinds—and workers to serve the workers—flocked in from all over Japan, bringing with them songs, dialects, and customs whose traces survive in the dances and festivals held in Aikawa today. But like other big-money booms, this one was short-lived. In less than thirty years, the richest and most accessible veins had already been exhausted.

Even so, there was still plenty of gold in Doyu-no-Wareto, and thirty years was long enough for the *bugyo*'s surveyors to have formed a good idea of where it was. Three hundred shafts were sunk, some as much as 2,500 feet below the surface of the

77

mountain. The main veins ran more or less parallel, separated by as little as 30 feet or as much as a couple of hundred, and each one had several minor veins running off from it. Some were of white quartz, in which the gold showed up as specks or streaks of black. The quartz, of course, had to be recovered with simple hand tools—hammers, picks, chisels, and wedges. Usually, such quartz deposits are surrounded by weak wall rock, but the rock of Doyu-no-Wareto, principally liparite and andesite, is unusually hard—bad news for the miners who had to hammer at the tunnel faces with crude iron tools, but at least relatively safe from the dangers of earthquakes. Another unusual feature was that the mountain contained two different types of deposit: the white quartz lodes, which occurred on the end of one main vein and in one branch vein, and a more common type in which the gold was embedded in a lead gray silver sulfate called argentite.

The proximity of a productive gold mine to a handy pool of political exiles and convicted criminals has led many to assume that Kinzan was worked more or less exclusively by slave labor. The mine is depicted as a hell of cold and damp where half-starved prisoners picked, shoveled, and clawed gold ore from the walls of freezing rock galleries until they shivered to death from pneumonia. This, at least, is a familiar part of the story that tour guides tell to the busloads of visitors they escort round Sado, and foreign writers, for whom the account dovetails neatly with wartime Japan's reputation for cold-blooded cruelty, have generally been content to give the same impression.

But although conditions inside the mountain were certainly bad, and must have cost many lives over the years, Kinzan was far too important an operation to have been entrusted to convicts. First, turning convicts into slaves was not as simple as it sounds: those who were on the island when the mine was discovered had already been tried and sentenced, and then as now, Japanese judicial decisions and conditions of detention could not easily be reviewed or altered. Second, and more to the point, mining for gold is much more technically complex

Heart of Gold

than, say, for coal. Relatively few kinds of work, even inside the mine, could be performed properly by unskilled slaves, since their incompetence, whether deliberate or not, might result in incomplete recovery of the precious deposits. Third, the rapid growth of Aikawa into a boom town, with its documented residential districts, bathhouses, shops, brothels, bars, and so on, makes it obvious that most of the workers were paid. And fourth, there is the surprising evidence of the water carriers' memorial.

Of the many technical problems inside the mine, one of the most persistent was flooding—and the deeper the operation descended into the mountain, the worse the problem became. Dozens of drainage tunnels were dug over the years, and these were fed by pumps that operated around the clock. The pumps were fantastic contraptions consisting of long cedarwood troughs, angled pipes made of sections of bamboo slotted together, and stubby little wooden handles that had to be cranked by hand. It was a monotonous, exhausting job and, in the early days, a well-paid one. Cash-hungry new arrivals literally queued up to do it. Later on, however, when output declined and the mine administrators sought ways to improve profitability, drainage work was an obvious area where costs could be cut. Homeless vagrants and others on the margins of society were arbitrarily arrested in big cities like Tokyo, Nagoya, and Osaka, ostensibly for reasons of "security," and sent to Sado to work as *mizukae ninsoku*, or "water carriers." The standard length of service was set at five years, after which they were to be released, but considering the cold, damp conditions in which they lived and worked, most can be assumed to have died before their time was up.

About two hundred yards down the valley from the main mine entrance, a footpath leads off up a slope and comes out on a flat terrace where there is a wooden statue and a stone memorial to the wretched water carriers. The inscription on the slab records that 1,800 of them died in the mine during the last hundred years of the Tokugawa shogunate. The figure may be arguable, but what is significant is that the matter is recorded at all: if Sado's resident population of exiles and convicts

79

had been regarded as a pool of free labor to be tapped as required, there would have been no need to press-gang innocent vagrants from distant cities, still less to erect a memorial recording their fate.

With effective pumping systems and techniques improved by experience, the Kinzan mine went on producing but never returned to the boom levels. In the fifteen years from 1688 to 1703, a serious effort was made to raise productivity, but the result was less than expected and enthusiasm flagged. Things declined even more when the shogunate was overthrown in 1868 and the country opened to foreign trade; Aikawa suffered immediate economic distress because gold could now be imported more cheaply than it could be produced by the primitive methods used on Sado. But the emperor intervened personally to avert calamity. Financial help was provided by the national government, and new foreign techniques were introduced, including the use of explosives and the first rock drills.

Kinzan's swansong began in 1918, when it was taken over by the Mitsubishi Mining Company. The new administration made an energetic start, quickly boosting the amount of ore extracted, but the payback was less than they hoped. Some records claim that in the early days, the most productive ores ran as high as 5,000 grams per metric ton, but by the twentieth century the very best did not exceed 500 grams and the average was more like 5.

Still, even 5 grams was better than nothing. From 1931 to 1943, placer operations were resumed on Aikawa's beach, with workers panning the alluvial deposits and picking through rocks and pebbles that had accumulated as old waste dumps. This beach placer had already been worked in the early days of the mine, but Japan's wartime need for cash made it worth sifting through the same deposits all over again. In 1940 alone, 189,787 metric tons of ore were recovered from the beach gravel, each yielding an average of 4.1 grams of gold and 73 grams of silver. Such was the "feverish zeal for gold" that Aikawa's beachside houses and the shore road behind them, which had been built on top of old dumps, were demolished to recover the low-grade

Heart of Gold

Wild flowers at Senkaku Bay

ore beneath. During these years, forced labor was certainly used: of the tens of thousands of Koreans imported to work for imperial Japan, more than 1,000 are known to have been sent to Sado. Of these, 145 are said to have "escaped" (but where to?) and a dozen or so—surely a low estimate—were killed. Their existence became public knowledge in 1991, after records were released of Mitsubishi's distribution of cigarette rations to its workers.

After the war, the U.S. Occupation forces conducted a study of gold and silver mining throughout Japan, and produced a report that made specific reference to operations in the Kinzan mine. The author, Robert Y. Grant, noted that hand drilling (with hammers and chisels) was still widely practiced, timbering was still done on an *ad hoc* basis, with even wedges rarely prepared in advance, and in general, safety was "poor, due to the indifference of both employees and management." Other comments from the report have a comparable ring of truth for people familiar with how things do and don't get

SADO: JAPAN'S ISLAND IN EXILE

done in modern Japanese companies. "It is in the field of exploration that Japanese gold- and silver-producing mines exhibit the smallest amount of progress," it states. "Outstanding geologists have published excellent papers on their studies but little or no use has been made of them by the mine operators. Mitsubishi, for instance, did not systematically assign geologists with geological duties to each mine until 1947." Elsewhere the report observes that in Japanese mines, a much smaller proportion of the workforce is engaged in actual production than is the rule in other countries. "The number of assistants, or helpers," its author notes dryly, "bulks large in comparison with, say, drill runners."

Now that operations have been abandoned, one tantalizing question remains: given the occurrence of such a vastly productive mine, isn't it likely that there is more gold to be found nearby? The true answer is "Not necessarily"—but that satisfies no one. Spurred on by visions of still more enormous wealth almost literally within its grasp, the Golden Sado Company, which presently owns the mine, has commissioned numerous geological surveys in the surrounding tangle of woods and mountains. To date, nothing exploitable has been found, and, although the company announced in 1988 that the search would be called off the following year, their brochure wistfully admits that "exploration of further gold is continuing."

* * *

The sky growled with menace and big raindrops spattered round me as I walked the last few hundred yards up the road to the mine. Just as I reached the entrance, the storm broke; I ran for cover under the long wooden bus shelter where a group of tourists were scrambling out of their coach, holding folded newspapers or plastic bags over their heads to protect them from the thrashing rain. A uniformed young woman in a little booth sold me an entrance ticket, which she handed over with a brochure in English and a map of the route I was to follow—without deviation, please—inside the mine.

The entrance tunnel was comfortably wide and high, so I

Heart of Gold

could easily stand up straight. Its floor was of smooth concrete, and along the rock walls hung a succession of colorful backlit displays giving statistical information about different stages in the mine's history, the numbers of workers, their various jobs, and the grades and quantities of gold they recovered. At the end of a long slope, the tunnel emerged into a large chamber with several shafts, passageways, and subchambers leading off it; the smallest of these, high off the ground, looked like the hollowed-out homes of giant woodpeckers. All the chambers contained mechanical models of human workers, acting out their various tasks with slow, robotlike movements to the recorded accompaniment of clanking wheels, banging hammers, and the shouts of overseers. One was chopping pit props with an ax, another hammering slowly at a chisel embedded in the rock face, another scooping water in a bucket and then tipping it out again, another sitting cross-legged on the ground with a notepad, keeping some kind of tally. To the sound of sloshing water, the water carriers cranked the handles of their archaic pumps. In one short tunnel a group of workers was supposed to be resting after their shift; some were lying asleep on the bare rock floor, using their folded forearms as pillows, while others squatted over bowls of food, miming the gestures of eating. One paused between each mouthful and turned his head, by means of a faintly squeaking hinge inside his neck, to look toward the spot where the tourists were gathered. It was an extraordinary scene, as technically ingenious as a mechanical zoo, and equally unrealistic. The intention was good but its execution ineffective, even laughable, as it might be if applied to a Chamber of Horrors in which supine plastic victims endured slow-motion cruelties at the hands of black-hooded robots while prerecorded shrieks and groans issued through stereo speakers; or to an erotic tableau showing stone-faced mannequins stiffly piston-pumping each other in complicated positions, their gasps of ecstasy compromised by electronic faults on the soundtrack.

Even so, there were details to be learned. The dummy workers lying on top of log platforms close to the roof, black-

83

smiths repairing tools, porters trudging along under heavy baskets, surveyors frowning at their plumb lines and scales, all gave some idea of the different tasks involved. Ventilation was provided by hand-operated bellows, light by oil lamps and paper candles. The atmosphere underground was cold and damp, even now in late May, and must have been worse still in winter, guaranteed to invite every respiratory disease in the book; yet the miners were dressed only in light cotton robes and straw sandals, with cloth turbans on their heads. The turbans were topped off with little straw mats, like beer coasters, tied under the chin with string and designed to offer some minimal protection from falling rocks or other objects—the only concession to individual safety that I could see.

The route from which I was not supposed to deviate led me out of the mine and into a museum, where the whole operation was re-created in miniature. In a glass case stood a model of the mountain, sliced through from top to bottom to show the network of tunnels. Inside were dozens of tiny workers clambering up and down ladders, pumping water, sorting ore, lighting lamps. It looked like an ant farm. At the foot of the mountain was a cavelike exit, beyond which lay a vast relief model of the whole valley, all the way down to the town of Aikawa and the sea. The open-fronted buildings were all roofed in traditional snow-country style, still seen on Sado's oldest houses, using overlapping shingles of cedar weighted down with stones. Inside them, workers were performing different jobs under the stern gaze of overseers dressed in samurai costume and girded with swords. First the ore was crushed, using an ingenious system based on a water-powered wheel: this turned a ratchet whose irregular spokes raised a line of heavy vertical hammers, one by one, and then dropped them onto the ore beneath. There were several smelters where the ore was heated in huge charcoal firepits by workers dressed only in loincloths; and after this, a succession of purification procedures that eventually produced long, sausage-shaped cylinders of gold. These were hammered flat into thin sheets and cut to a manageable size with large secateurs; then they were melted,

Heart of Gold

cooled, hammered out, and cut up yet again until their purity was deemed sufficient for them to be made into the ultimate product, the *koban* coins. Each stage of the operation was supervised by armed guards and was provided with an adjoining room for its own administrative department. Here a small army of clerks kept the records, seated on tatami floors with their weights, measures, scales, brushes, ink, and ledger books spread out on low tables in front of them.

The road down the valley passed through several security checkpoints on its way into the streets of Aikawa, where more model buildings attempted to show something of the life of the town. There were spacious houses with broad verandahs lit by colored paper lanterns, where off-duty workers lounged around drinking while girls entertained them with music. There were eating shops and gambling joints, a public bathhouse, a temple and several stalls set up along the streets to sell fish, vegetables, clothes, and tools. Although the model was not realistic, it gave a good idea of relative scale and clearly showed that operations outside the mine were far more complex and occupied far more workers than what took place inside the mountain.

It was still raining when I came out of the museum, and to judge by the leaden sky overhead, the rain looked well set in for the rest of the day. I would have liked to wander around Aikawa, which, although a dull-looking town even in fine weather, contains many well-preserved temples and shrines as well as curious reminders of its odd history. Some of its streets and districts, recalling the long-ago presence of exiled nobles from the old imperial court, are named like those of Kyoto—Nakagyo-cho ("Middle Street") or Shimogyo-cho ("Lower Street"), for instance—while others reflect the grouping together of trades and occupations, such as Daiku-cho ("Carpenter"), Yaoya-cho ("Grocer"), and Misoya-cho ("Miso-maker"). Other well-known sights in Aikawa include the temple Daijo-ji, burial place of the mother of Ryokan, a famous Zen hermit, poet, and calligrapher; Daian-ji, a temple dedicated to Okubo Nagayasu, Sado's first *bugyo;* Oyamazumi, a shrine built in 1605 to the god of the Kinzan

85

SADO: JAPAN'S ISLAND IN EXILE

mountain; and high on a hill above the town, the sacred lair of Futatsuiwa ("Two Rocks") Danzaburo, Sado's most famous *mujina* trickster-badger.

Despite the rain, I decided to make a detour to the Futatsuiwa shrine. Unlike its decaying counterpart in Seki, which I had explored the day before, it was carefully maintained and obviously still in regular use. The *torii* gates that made up the long tunnel from the entrance to the shrine must have numbered more than a hundred. They had been presented by adherents from all over the country, and each one had the name and hometown of its donor inscribed with brush and ink. The shrine itself wore a brand new coat of gleaming red paint.

Tradition holds that Danzaburo was Sado's "boss" *mujina,* maintaining contact with and authority over his comrades elsewhere on the island. One story tells that whenever a ship came down from the coastal villages further north, Danzaburo would change himself into a woman, don a straw hat, and go to the docks with a package, which he would ask the crew to carry, unopened, to his friend Sabuto, the resident *mujina* at Seki. The return journey to Seki was an easy one (before the prevailing southerly wind), so the crew could look forward to relaxing along the way. On one trip, however, their curiosity led them to open the package and eat the grapes and *akebi* (a kind of mountain banana) that they found inside. Moments later the wind changed, and the ship was wrecked with the loss of all hands.

Danzaburo's special claim to fame was his habit of lending money. Humans in need of a loan would write down the amount and proposed date of repayment on a piece of paper, sign with their name and seal, and leave it beside the *mujina*'s lair. If he felt inclined to grant the loan, the borrower would find the money waiting for him in the same place the following morning. But over the years, the number of borrowers increased, and many failed to make repayment, so that eventually Danzaburo stopped lending. Another expression of the same generous spirit, paralleled in numerous *wankashi densetsu* ("bowl-lending" legends) from all over Japan, had Danzaburo loaning bowls, cups, trays, and other domestic articles; but this

Heart of Gold

practice also was abandoned when too many people failed to return them. Sometimes, it was said, a curious human would clamber down into the lair and follow a tunnel leading to a sumptuous palace where he would find Danzaburo and his family wearing fine clothes and seated at a long table loaded with delicious food. When (and if) they emerged, such adventurers would find themselves victims of a supernatural distortion of time, three days in Danzaburo's palace being the equivalent of three years in the human world.

By now soaked through and footsore, I trudged down into Aikawa and took a room for the night at an inn. The owner accepted me with some reluctance, as though he were used to a better class of customer than wet and weary foot travelers, but could not quite find it in himself to turn me away. I was given a gloomy little room whose window faced the grimy wall of the next-door building, close enough to touch; but I was too tired to care. A hot bath made me feel better, and when the maid came in with the dinner, I was watching the television news. The lead story for the day was about the weather, which was analyzed in detail and then diagnosed as "changeable." After that came a story about a bunch of local bureaucrats wearing identical dark suits, bowing repeatedly to each other, and approving the route of a new road. I switched off the set and turned to the food. It was dull and poorly prepared. The rice was actually cold, something I had never come across in Japan before. Just at that moment there was a tremendous burst of noise: a karaoke party was just starting up in a room across the corridor. "How long will that be going on?" I asked the maid. She bowed deeply and apologized for the inconvenience. "They have booked the room until ten o'clock," she said. "After that, I'm sure it will stop." She didn't sound sure at all. The singing was interrupted by an almighty crash, followed by cheers, clapping, and laughter, as though someone had fallen over a table. "I am so sorry," said the maid again as she backed out of the door.

I decided to abandon the dinner and go out into Aikawa for something to eat. The first place I tried had a large red

87

SADO: JAPAN'S ISLAND IN EXILE

lantern hanging outside and clouds of charcoal-scented smoke billowing out of a small ventilator. Ducking past the half-length curtain in the doorway, I found myself in a small, shabby *yakitori-ya*, or chicken kebab shop. The owner and his wife were red in the face from drinking, but welcomed me cheerfully without breaking off from what they were doing. Two large plates lay on the counter, piled with ready-to-go *yakitori*, and more was cooking on the two grills. Even so, they regretted that they couldn't serve me any, since it had all been ordered by a hotel along the street. One of the hotel's employees was hanging around with an air of impatience, and I wondered if this was an order from the karaoke party I had just escaped from. I asked for bean curd, as this needed no cooking and would give my puffing, panting hosts the minimum of trouble. The wife handed me a nutty-tasting bowlful and, after a few minutes, a stick of *yakitori* made of some strange meat I didn't recognize—white, wrinkly skin on one side and little gobbets of flesh on the other. It was tough and gristly, and while I tried to eat it, the woman tried to explain what it was. *"Buta, buta,"* she said. Okay, pig. Some part of a pig. "Baby," put in the husband, using the English word. He leaned across and patted his wife's abdomen. "Baby place." The light dawned. It was pig's womb. I laid the stick down and went back to the bean curd. Soon another customer came in and barked an order that I didn't catch. They served him a large plate filled with raw onion rings and a sloppy mess of bloody uncooked offal that looked like—"Same, same," said the owner, addressing me. Raw onion and raw pig's womb. I paid up and left.

At the other end of the street was a sushi shop. I sat at the counter and let the owner, who was intrigued to have a foreigner in the place, take me on a guided tour of his stock. We got talking about *fugu*, globefish, which are plentiful in the sea around Sado. He asked if I wanted to try some. I declined as politely as possible. *Fugu* can only be prepared and served by restaurateurs with a special license, because some of its organs contain a poison that can kill the eater if they are not completely removed. Japanese gourmets consider it a great delicacy, and I've always felt they're welcome to it.

88

Heart of Gold

Tunnel of torii *at the shrine of Danzaburo, near Aikawa*

Even a whole lifetime isn't long enough to sample every food in the world, and I'm content to miss out all the ones that contain deadly toxins. But the shop owner wasn't going to take no for an answer. The globefish was on the house. "It's wonderful," he assured me. "You're going to love it." I glanced around, searching for some diversion to change the subject. There were only two other customers in the shop, two women facing each other over a small table in the corner. One was staring vacantly into space while the other, with the mirror of her open powder compact held close to her face, was picking shreds of food out from the gaps between her yellow and silver teeth.

An old wooden clock behind the counter began to strike the hour. At the same moment, the shop owner's wife emerged from the kitchen with two grilled *fugu* on a plate, which she set down in front of me with a smile of triumph. There was no way to refuse. It seemed insane to die for the sake of good manners—a peculiarly English fate—but by and large I had had a happy life and had greatly enjoyed my final few days, walking around Sado. Here was as good a place as any for the curtain to come down. I picked up the chopsticks, separated a section of the soft white flesh, and put it into my mouth. Nothing happened. There wasn't anything unusual about the taste, either. *This* was the great delicacy? I finished the two *fugu* while the

89

SADO: JAPAN'S ISLAND IN EXILE

shop owner regarded me with an air of unconcern. "You see?" he said. "It's all right, isn't it? We sell a lot of that. There's nothing to worry about."

"Even so," I said, "some people die in Japan every year from eating it, don't they?"

"Not in this shop," he answered simply.

At that moment, the door opened and three men came in. Already quite drunk, they seated themselves a little way down the counter from me and shouted for beer. Presently, the one nearest to me looked round and noticed something strange in his favorite sushi shop. "Hey!" he cried. "What's this? American! Hey, you! Me Japanese!" He touched the tip of his nose with his forefinger, so that I should know who he was referring to. "Me Yamamoto! Me Sado!" The man next to him pulled gently at his shoulder to shut him up, but Mr. Yamamoto shrugged him roughly away. "Hey, you GI, hey . . ." He paused, forgetting what he wanted to say. Then it came back. "America no good," he said sternly. "Japan good, America no good."

"You could be right," I replied evenly. "I hardly know the place."

This wasn't in the script. Mr. Yamamoto gaped stupidly, his mouth hanging open. He stank of whisky.

"He's not American," said the shop owner. "He's from England. You got that wrong, didn't you?"

His opening gambit having backfired, Mr. Yamamoto felt embarrassed. He also realized he had been rude. It was time to buy me a beer. As we drank, he told me his story. As a young man, he had left Sado and gone to Tokyo to find work. He had hated it, living in squalid lodgings, laboring in jobs where pay and work availability were controlled by gangsters, despised by the city boys for his uncouth manners, laughed at for his country accent. "But I stayed," he said, with a touch of pride. "I stayed for fifteen years. And then one day, I knew I'd had enough. I just knew. I wanted to come home. So I quit my job and back I came!" He looked at me with an air of defiance.

"So what do you do now?" I asked him.

"Anything! I do anything! Woodwork, roofing, farming, a

90

Heart of Gold

bit of fishing—anything. I don't care, because I'm back here. This is my home. I was born here, I'll die here. My children, they want to leave. When school is over, they want to go to Tokyo. 'Go to Tokyo, then,' I tell them. I've been there. I'm not going again. I want to stay right here."

I felt glad for him. Drunk as he was, he conveyed the frustration of life in Tokyo very clearly—screwing up his face at the thought of it, raising his voice, bunching his shoulders, clenching his hands, jerking his head. But when he reached the part about giving it up and coming back to Sado, his whole body relaxed, his gestures became wide and sweeping, he tossed his head and laughed, his eyes sparkled. He must have been in his late forties, with no trade, no steady employment, no idea what job he would do after the present one was finished. What's more, he didn't care. *I do anything!* Cured of city-worship, he was home for good. If there was a job around, he was ready to do it. If not, he stayed in bed, or got drunk. Whichever it was, he was happy.

DAY 4 | AMONG THE EXILES

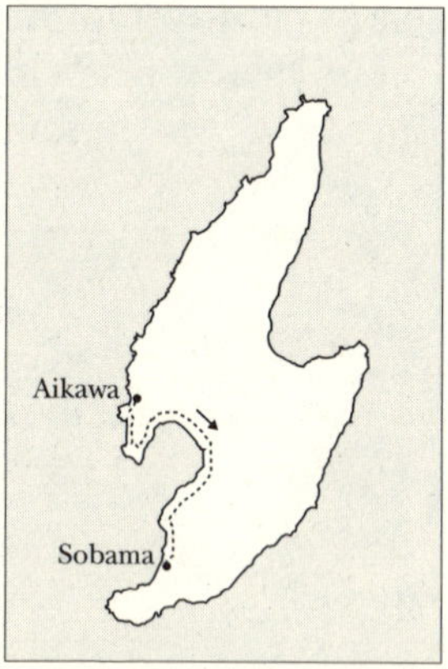

Oka Genzaburo chose a beautiful spot to commit suicide. A samurai from Echigo province, he had fought in one of the long-running clan wars that used to punctuate life in medieval Japan and had ended up on the losing side. With most of his clan wiped out and his lord captured, Oka Genzaburo had no options left but death by *seppuku,* or self-disembowelment. So he set off to return home, intending to say farewell to his family and do the deed on familiar ground. But his enemies got there first; by the time he arrived the house was burnt down and there was no sign of his wife and children. In a final, futile gesture of defiance, he escaped across the sea to Sado, made his way to Aikawa, and thence to Kasugamisaki, the first headland south of the town. Here, all alone on the grassy tip of a narrow promontory that juts sharply out into the sea like the point of an arrow, he sat and waited for the dawn, then cut open his abdomen with a dagger and died.

My visit to the sushi bar the night before had involved

92

Among the Exiles

more beer than originally intended, and when I stumbled up to Kasugamisaki in the early hours of the following morning, it seemed a good place to stop and clear my head. There was a stiff wind blowing off the sea, and I stood on Oka Genzaburo's grassy knoll and took several deep breaths while watching the long, foam-tipped breakers roll steadily in and smash into the black rocks below. It was a wild, desolate-looking shore, with more than a touch of the west coast of Ireland, and the sense of confronting the very limit of the world was sharpened by the low roar of the wind as it rushed through the long, tussocky grass. Close by was a memorial to the dead hero, a four-sided stone structure that rose to a narrow platform topped off by a stone lantern. I took my camera out of the pack and composed a photograph of it that would capture the drama of the setting, with plenty of sea and coastline in the background. After carefully packing the camera away again, I turned round and discovered that the real memorial was behind me, a big mound marked with a slab of smooth granite on which was carved Oka Genzaburo's name. The lantern, as I should have guessed from its position on the cliff edge, was exactly what it looked like—a lantern, probably once used as a warning beacon.

Kasugamisaki marks the beginning of a stubby little peninsula that extends to the southernmost point of O-Sado and forms one arm of Mano Bay, the long, sheltered crescent of beach on the west side of the island's central plain. The interior of this peninsula is rugged and undeveloped except for a few rice paddies, and the shore is punctuated with long, shoestring villages built along the narrow strip of land between the base of the cliffs and the edge of the sea. Even a century ago, some of these villages were more than a mile long and in one place, near the tip of the peninsula, the road passed between a double line of houses that extended without a break for seven miles. Away from the central plain, virtually all Sado's settlements are on the coast, and are outgrowths of the same original design— long and narrow in form and only occasionally including two or three other streets, parallel to the through road, where the cliffs stand far enough back from the sea to provide the neces-

93

SADO: JAPAN'S ISLAND IN EXILE

Stone lantern at Kasugamisaki, near Aikawa

sary space. With the shoreline road as its only accessible part, the peninsula as a whole is known as Nanaura Kaigan, or "Seven Bays Coast."

Modern engineering, however, has been employed to modify these traditional arrangements, as the road through the old villages is in many places too narrow and twisty for tourist buses to pass through. Most of the villages are now bypassed by a new road cut out of the mountainsides above them. The local people are probably delighted, but strangers on foot find it confusing because they can easily pass by a village without realizing it is there at all.

A sudden squall of rain sent me scurrying for cover under the eaves of an old farmhouse. I waited in silence, hoping that the people it belonged to would stay sensibly indoors until the weather cleared up and not come out to discover a foreign

Among the Exiles

lunatic flattening himself against the side of their home at seven o'clock in the morning. Despite the brisk rain and the clouds scudding across the sky, the sun was doing its best to come out; I could see a brilliant rainbow arching into the sea behind a grove of pine trees. Looking around at the cultivated fields close to the house, I also noticed how much darker and richer the soil was here than further north. The landscape had more and bigger trees, including figs in fruit, and a wider variety of vegetables: broad beans, french beans, peas, tomatoes, spring onions, lettuce, cabbage, carrots, and eggplant could all be seen from where I was standing.

Setting off as soon as the rain stopped, I rounded the first corner and discovered a signpost informing me that I had missed the village of Oura, but was now entering Takase, its immediate neighbor. Takase's tourist attraction was a pair of large gray rocks at one end of the beach, called Husband Rock and Wife Rock. They stood side by side like twins, miniature mountains with the same conical shape and a few scattered patches of green lichens on their flanks. Husband Rock was solid, while Wife Rock had a long vertical gash right through from one side to the other, offering an oval window on the open sea beyond and a piece of natural symbolism comprehensible to even the dimmest tourist. They made a picturesque sight, in a postcardy sort of way, and were the reason for a big hotel and restaurant complex on the same beach, with a fifteen-slot coach park. Inside, a group of tourists were already getting up strength for the day with a hearty breakfast while their driver was busy outside cleaning his coach with a bucket of soapy water and an instrument like a windscreen wiper on the end of a long bamboo pole.

The next hamlet was another with a bypass, but this time I was ready for it. Taking the old road down toward the sea, I found myself in a gray, weather-beaten village with a single winding street bordered by dark, irregular wooden houses whose upper stories, supported by heavy wooden pillars, jutted out above the ground floor. In some places, they leaned close enough together for a neighborly cup of rice to be passed from

95

SADO: JAPAN'S ISLAND IN EXILE

one side of the street to the other. Dozens of swallows were flitting backward and forward between the great outdoors and their half-built nests in the eaves.

The village had no beach to speak of, only a jumble of rocks at the sea edge below a sturdy concrete wall. A few yards out to sea was a low rock stack with a tiny shrine perched on top of it, and at its foot stood an old woman in rubber waders and a red headscarf. Up to her thighs in the water, she was hauling away at floating clumps of seaweed with a wooden rake and stuffing them into a large basket slung across her shoulders with a white rope. The choppy sea didn't seem to bother her, even though the waves were surging round her and threatening to knock her off balance.

Across the street from the seawall was another shrine, much bigger and completely bundled up with straw matting. It looked as though someone was halfway through gift wrapping it, intending to send it to an old friend through the mail. I went up to it, lifted the edge of one of the mats, and peeped in to see what was going on. The shrine had deteriorated somewhat, due to age and weathering, but still retained all its elaborate carvings of magic birds and snorting dragons and didn't appear to have anything seriously wrong with it. Around its sides was a sturdy scaffold of old pine logs lashed together. The crosspieces were long, thick bamboo poles, and the tightly woven straw mats, long enough to reach from the top of the roof all the way to the ground, were tied onto the scaffold with string. They formed a sort of giant coat, blocking out the weather completely. Perhaps the shrine was being dried out before having some preservative applied to the timbers. Whatever the reason, it was wonderfully warm and snug in there; outside, the wind was still coming off the sea at a brisk clip, but not a breath came through the curtain of heavy mats. If it had been the end of the day instead of the beginning, I would have been tempted to lay out my sleeping bag on the shrine's verandah and stay for the night.

Beyond the village, the road resumed bypass mode and climbed back up the mountainside. Soon it emerged onto a

96

Among the Exiles

plateau that had been divided into a network of small paddies separated from each other by low, narrow embankments. Ten or twelve figures were standing around, up to their ankles in water, and I stopped to watch them at work. But whatever they were doing, there was evidently no hurry: they just stood there, looking at the fields, as though undecided about which task to tackle next. Then the penny dropped—they were not people, but scarecrows. One was dressed in bright red pajamas and a battered old lampshade hat, another in blue trousers and a white shirt, a third in the remnants of a dark brown suit. Their heads were made of cardboard, or silvery colored sacking, shaded by hats or bound with headscarves, and several had crude, Halloween pumpkin faces painted on both sides. Dangling from the ends of their outstretched arms were various bird-scaring devices—plastic bags shredded into strips, stiff plastic flags, rusty bells dangling from wire loops, colored umbrellas, or red and silver metallic streamers twisted to catch the sun. Apart from these flapping accessories they were still, and their stillness gave them a sinister, almost menacing air. A solitary scarecrow may be a scarecrow, nothing more, but this group seemed to share some consciousness beyond their innocent function as deceivers of birds. They stood like waiting presences in league with the unseen, ghostly incarnations of Sado's benevolent magic, these servants of Sohodoro-na-kami, god of scarecrows and protector of the fields.

* * *

Having crossed the plateau of rice paddies, the road began to wind back down the mountainside toward the sea. Occasional breaks in the trees gave a view over Kuninaka, Sado's central plain, the whole wide sweep of Mano Bay, and beyond, to the southern half of the island and the yellow sand at far-off Sobama Beach, which I aimed to reach by nightfall. At the foot of the hill, where the plain began, my road turned right, along the coast and through Sawada and Mano, two towns that have grown into one and now make up the biggest urban settlement on the island. But first I had a detour to make.

97

SADO: JAPAN'S ISLAND IN EXILE

A little way inland from Sawada are two temples associated with a powerful Buddhist sect whose founder was a thirteenth-century priest named Nichiren. A combative man of fiercely held opinions, Nichiren was exiled to Sado for persistent public criticism of the government and for making outspoken attacks on rival sects of Buddhism. Something of the same antagonistic attitude still animates the Nichiren sect today; it is regarded with bug-eyed devotion by its adherents and with something between discomfort and distaste by everyone else. Like Mormons or Jehovah's Witnesses, contemporary followers are seen by outsiders as aggressively evangelistic, cliquish, and irritatingly self-satisfied. At the same time. their lay organization is populous and wealthy, and while the modern message is universalist—"May Peace Prevail On Earth" is a favorite slogan—the posture is right-wing, authoritarian, and sharply focused on adulation of the current leader. It seems unfair to blame Nichiren for this situation, seven hundred years after his death, but people do; his name still arouses pretty much the same emotions, for and against, as when he was alive.

After an initial period of deprivation on Sado, Nichiren was "adopted" by a sympathizer and allowed to live at his home. This place is now a temple complex called Myosho-ji, complete with ornate gardens, gateways, tall slabs of stone inscribed with quotations from the master, and clear pools of water planted with lilies and spanned by tiny stone bridges. But Myosho-ji lies enclosed by trees in a hollow on the mountainside, with no view in any direction, so every morning, it's said, the exile would walk half a mile down the track to the edge of a steep escarpment overlooking the Kuninaka plain. Here he would perform his devotions as the sun rose over the mountain ridge to the east and flooded the plain with light.

A second temple, Jisso-ji, now stands on this escarpment, and I spent some time exploring the grounds. In the middle of a large graveled area bordered by neat flowerbeds stood a massive statue of Nichiren set up on a concrete plinth. The plinth was inscribed, in English and Japanese, with the words "May Peace Prevail On Earth."

Among the Exiles

The statue showed a tough, stocky man with a craggy face, hands clasped together, beads slung over his left wrist, and dressed in a kimono covered by a short coat. As I was studying it, I was approached by the temple guardian, a garrulous old woman who launched without introduction into a rapid account of Nichiren's life and history. Didn't I think he was an amazing man? Did I know that he worked miracles? Had I studied his doctrines? Did I realize that thousands of devotees came here as pilgrims every year? And finally, seeing that I made no answer, did I understand what she was saying? "No," I told her amiably, to shut her up, "hardly a word."

Here as elsewhere, the striking feature of temples dedicated to Nichiren is the enormous care, effort, and expense undertaken to make them look impressive—not just the immaculate gardens, but the temple interiors with their lavish gold ornamentation, the extravagant use of lacquer, the glittering statuary, the plaster angels, the elaborately carved throne. This is not a form of Buddhism that delights in the ordinary, but one that seeks to elevate. It's as though association with the simple preoccupations of simple people risks lowering the leader in the eyes of his followers, as though he could be made more glorious by a vigorous personality cult placing him at the Right Hand of God the Father Almighty. The followers apparently find it convincing, but for the uninitiated it looks tasteless and vulgar, as if Christians, in telling the story of the nativity, sought to give it a bit of spurious gloss by re-siting it in the Tiberius Suite at the Bethlehem Hilton. Yet no attempt is made to hide the fact that Nichiren was on Sado as an exile. His privations are remembered with pride. And here on the Kuninaka plain, Nichiren was in exalted company; banishment to Sado was a fate shared at various times by aristocrats, generals, ecclesiastics, artists, and even emperors.

Exile has a long history in Japan and, like the expulsion of Adam and Eve from the Garden of Eden, traces its authority to divine precedent. According to an early history called the *Kojiki* (Record of Ancient Matters), the dispositions made by the country's original creator, the god Izanagi, included directing

99

his capricious son Susa-no-wo to assume responsibility for the tides, currents, and living creatures of the oceans; but the son had other plans and set off instead to visit the land of his mother, leaving the "mountains to wither away and the rivers and seas to dry up." In anger at this disobedience, his father expelled him from the High Celestial Plain with "a divine expulsion."

Before the coming of Buddhism to Japan in the seventh century, serious crimes were normally punished by death, but contemporary Chinese historical records mention that their island neighbors made frequent use of banishment and flogging as well. The first systematic code of Japanese law, which was promulgated in 668, specified three grades of *tsuiho,* or banishment—near, medium, and far—for different degrees of offense. Much later, in feudal times, the shogunate's stricter social regime extended these categories to seven, ranging from *tokoro-barai,* which barred the criminal only from his own village or community, to a kind of blanket ban that expelled him from all the fifteen provinces around Edo and Kyoto and, for good measure, denied him the use of major highways as well. Persons condemned to death could also have their sentences commuted to banishment as a result of intervention by influential third parties. Islands, which offered security as well as isolation, were ideal destinations, and Sado's first exile, a poet called Hozumia-son-no-oi, arrived as early as the year 722.

As Buddhist influence continued to grow, particularly the belief that the ghost of an executed person could return to exact revenge, use of the death penalty as a judicial instrument declined. In fact from 818 to 1156, it was abolished altogether, although lawbreakers still faced other severe punishments. Exile became the maximum sentence, and not only for transgressions of the law: individuals who fell from official favor could be effectively banished by being appointed to some post in a distant province. Others became exiles by choice, to put themselves and their families beyond the reach of powerful enemies.

In 1185, the Heian Period ended and authority passed

Among the Exiles

*Statue of Nichiren
at Jisso-ji*

from the imperial court into the hands of the military clans, who were much less squeamish about taking life. Common law was strict and categories of criminals were numerous. But for Japan's robbers, pickpockets, murderers, arsonists, rapists, adulterers, blackmailers, and disturbers of public order, plenty of harsh summary punishments were available. Relatively few such people were reckoned to merit the extra administrative work involved in dispatching and supervising an exile. The new growth area was the category of political exiles, once-powerful individuals removed for backing a wrong horse, for ideological deviation, or for belonging to outlawed sects or organizations. Far from being tough, street-hardened villains, these were often persons of culture and education, well-born, intellectual, with artistic or professional skills. No wonder that when they arrived at their place of exile they weren't feared or scorned, but admired and respected as bringers of new knowledge.

Exiles were allowed a good deal of freedom within their assigned area. The highest classes (certainly a small minority) could even bring goods and servants with them, build homes, and pass their time much as they liked. Although they were supposed to work for local people, doing fishing and farming chores, in practice they lived however they could. Such freedom of choice was forbidden, but the rule was ignored, so that remote, backward Sado had a more or less permanent pool of teachers, actors, and musicians as well as craftsmen like masons, carpenters, and builders.

SADO: JAPAN'S ISLAND IN EXILE

Sometimes, exiles were allowed to bring their children with them (to protect them from dangerous enemies, for instance), but wives were almost always banned. This led to many taking island mistresses, known as *mizukumi-onna* ("water-drawing women") because liaisons commonly began when the women helped out with domestic chores. The unions were not binding, however long they lasted, and such rights as existed were in the exile's favor: when his sentence was over, he could decide whether or not to take his island "wife" and children with him. If he chose, and some did, he could just take the children and leave the "wife" behind.

With this degree of social freedom, acts of violence were rare. So were attempts at escape, since failure meant death and failure was almost certain. Nevertheless, some still tried. One of the strongest motives was pure despair, since the duration of an exile's sentence was decided at the trial but not disclosed to him, the government preferring to keep its sentencing policy for different offenses known only to a few high officials. Others chanced escape out of resentment at an unjust conviction, or the obligation to repay a blood debt.

But most of Sado's exiles had a full-time job just staying warm and getting enough to eat. Food was short even for the islanders, and new arrivals without land to plant or skills to gather often went hungry. What was available was poor in quality: there were a few starchy root species, a notorious soup based on seawater, and rough gruels made from pounded millet, barley, or vegetables. Sweet potatoes, which grow well even in poor soil, were not introduced until the early eighteenth century. Rice would have been a rare treat, probably available only at festivals and even then only to the rich and privileged. Edible wild plants were another possible food source, and so were the fruits of the sea; but sometimes, in their ignorance of local conditions, exiles sickened on poisonous berries or slipped off slick wet rocks and drowned while foraging on the shore in bad weather.

It was midmorning now, and I was getting hungry myself, so I walked back to Sawada to find something to eat. The main street ran parallel to the shore and was lined with nondescript

Among the Exiles

shops. At a small, dusty little grocery store I bought some rice balls, a couple of apples, and a small bag of cherries. The old woman at the till, observing my stick, warned me off the mountains. "Take care if you go up there," she said. "The weather today could turn nasty—please make sure to come back safely." This sounded like good advice, so I carried my purchases down to the beach, and ate them sitting on the sand as the wind gusted around me and blew wreaths of murky colored cloud on and off the tops of the distant mountains.

Someone else who spent time on this beach at Sawada, and described it in his *Kintosho* (Book of the Golden Island), was another famous exile, Zeami. Zeami was one of the founding geniuses of Japan's Noh theater, a brilliant actor, playwright, and critic who was born into a distinguished Kyoto family in 1363. As a teenager, he became a protege of the ruling shogun, who encouraged the boy's education and advised him to make a study of Zen. He is credited with having written about ninety Noh plays, including several that were rewrites of earlier pieces, and such critical works as the seven-part *Fushi Kaden* (Transmission of the Flower of Acting Style) and *Shikadosho* (Essay on the Way to the Flower). Zeami often used the term "flower" to denote the invisible genius of performance, the ability to act out something familiar yet make the audience feel and see it as if for the first time.

Zeami dominated the development of Noh theater until 1422, when he retired and took up the contemplative life of a Soto Zen monk. The theatrical mantle passed to his gifted elder son, Motomasa. Soon afterward, things began to go wrong. A new shogun took power and made known his preference for the Noh interpretations of Zeami's nephew, a man called On'ami. Zeami and Motomasa were barred from the shogun's court, and when Motomasa died in 1432, On'ami became supreme in the world of Noh. Two years later, Zeami was banished to Sado. The precise charge is not known, but he may have angered the shogun by disdaining the nephew who had supplanted his beloved son. Some believe that he died on the island, others that he returned eventually to Kyoto.

103

SADO: JAPAN'S ISLAND IN EXILE

Coincidentally, Sado itself has long been closely associated with Noh, more closely than almost any part of Japan. This has less to do with Zeami than with the discovery of gold at Aikawa and the government's dispatch of Okubo Nagayasu to take charge of its exploitation. The Okubos were a family of actors, and the newly appointed *bugyo* brought a troupe of performers with him as part of his entourage. With its dramatic recitals and subtle, mannered enactments of scenes from famous tales and legends, Noh caught on in a big way. Before long, villages all over Sado were competing among themselves to build their own stages and put on their own plays. To cover the costs, each village set aside the income derived from one community-owned rice field. This system lasted until after World War II, when government reforms lumped the old irregular landholdings together and then redistributed them among the former tenants. This undermined the financing system, pushing Noh into decline and posing the danger that it might one day disappear from Sado altogether. For the moment, tradition is holding the line and there are still 30 or 40 stages in active use. These are all that remain from a onetime total of over 200 and compares instructively with present-day Tokyo, where there are 10. Tokyo's theaters, of course, are in modern buildings with comfortable padded seats, electric lights, coffee lounges, and shops where patrons can buy copies of the text of the play they have come to see, plus fans, cushions, and anything else they can be persuaded to need. Sado's stages are all in the open air, as they always used to be, with the audience sitting on mats on the ground.

* * *

Flicking the last few cherry stones into the gutter along the way, I left the beach and headed on through the town. It was a dull sort of place, not much more than a shopping center, but one building, a whitewashed, half-timbered house, caught my eye. At roof height, a large signboard inscribed "Obata Shuzo" announced the place as a sake brewery. I went inside and found Mr. Obata himself, a balding, fit-looking man in his mid-fifties. To judge from the decor, he seemed anxious to present not

104

Among the Exiles

only an excellent product but also evidence of his acquaintance with the great and famous. The walls were hung with framed color photos of him meeting this and that dignitary, politician, and royal personage. The biggest one was of him kissing the hand of the Pope.

As a rare foreign visitor I was taken under his wing and treated to a tour of the premises, where huge vatfuls of fermenting rice were being thoughtfully stirred amid clouds of steam by serious-looking men armed with wooden paddles. There was more to interest me when the tour ended up in the tasting room, where tiny samples were poured out from several bottles for the appraisal of a foreign palate. A few of these bottles had something that looked like a snake curled up at the bottom, and so it proved: some islanders, including Mr. Obata, use the standard commercial product as the base for a powerful home brew called *mamushi-zake,* taken now and again as a pick-me-up, restorer of flagging male potency, and general cure-all. The method is simple: just catch a *mamushi* (adder), and pickle it in ordinary sake for a year. Then drink the sake and shift the *mamushi* to a fresh bottle. One medium-size *mamushi* is good for up to three years' brewing.

From the doorway of his brewery, Mr. Obata pointed down the road toward Yawata, a place he seemed determined I should visit. Yawata is one of many alternative names for the Shinto sword-god Hachiman; according to Zeami's *Book of the Golden Island,* there was once an important shrine there. Today the site of the old shrine is occupied by a large modern hotel set back from the road among a stand of red pines. As I passed by it began to rain, so I ran for shelter under the archway of the building next door, which turned out to be the Sado Museum.

The archway led through to a garden containing half a dozen old buildings that had been taken down at their original sites and reassembled here. One was an old farmhouse, thickly thatched, with a gable window looking out from the upstairs storage area and a ground floor that visitors could go inside and explore. Held up by massive beams and pillars of cedar, the silent, faintly dust-scented interior was built to an open-plan

105

SADO: JAPAN'S ISLAND IN EXILE

design with no doors except those to the outside. The kitchen was filled with traditional implements, including ladles, a giant mallet, and two or three tubs for pounding rice to make the chewy derivative called *mochi*. There was also a firepit sunk in the floor with a black iron kettle suspended above the powdery ashes on a bamboo contraption with iron levers to adjust the height.

Inside the museum, the exhibits were jumbled together without much organization. The portrayal of Sado's early history was vague, with a dramatic tableau showing the island's geological formation amidst volcanic explosions and heaving seas and another depicting naked, panic-stricken primitives running in terror from a forest engulfed by flames. These imaginative works were balanced by one very definite fact in the shape of a skeleton labeled *Desmostylus mirabilis nagao,* evidently some prehistoric creature. About the size of a baby elephant, it was eight or ten feet long from nose to tail, stood about four feet at the shoulder, and had an enormous rib cage, which looked easily big enough to accommodate two, or even three, well-chewed human adults. Other animals on display belonged to more recent times: there was a colossal eagle with eyes as big as coat buttons, various stuffed birds and snakes, a few stoats and weasels, and two different species of *tanuki,* the shapechanger. One was a woolly looking little fellow like a puppy with pale fur fringing a black nose and dark eyes surrounded by haloes of dark hairs which made them look huge. The other type had long, soft, fluffy fur and was the size of a cat, although with sharper features—a fox-cat, maybe. This collection of creatures stood side by side in a glass cabinet across from a display of theatrical masks. One glowered back at them with particular intensity; it was a Noh mask, portraying a very old man with thick eyebrows, long gray hair, a straggly white horsehair beard, and a zanily colored cloth draped over his head. On top of the cloth was a black hat shaped like an inverted Wellington boot. The vacant eye sockets added a final touch: the mask looked like the stoned-out distillation of a thousand rock festival veterans.

A little way up the road was another museum, better orga-

106

Among the Exiles

nized and, to judge by the size of the parking area, more attuned to the interests of contemporary visitors. This was Toki-no-Sato, named after the Japanese crested ibis, a plump, ungainly, slow-stepping bird with a long, red, down-curving beak and vivid pink flight feathers. Once indigenous to Sado it is now right on the edge of extinction, as attempts to get the last surviving pair to breed have so far failed. Instead, visitors can buy a life-size plastic *toki* in the souvenir shop, or else an ashtray, dishcloth, paperweight, or T-shirt bearing its picture.

The upstairs floor of Toki-no-Sato was devoted to the work of Shodo Sasaki, a wonderfully talented artist who was born in Sawada in 1882. As a young man, he left the island and traveled to Tokyo to study painting but was forced by health problems to return a few years later. He then apprenticed himself to a local teacher and became expert in wax casting, a technique in which a pattern is first made with beeswax and then covered with clay. The wax is then melted away to leave a finished mold. Using this system, the artist produced a huge body of work as daring and inventive as anything by his famous contemporaries in Europe: super-realistic rabbits and birds in ceramic and bronze, enamel deer with strange arcane designs on their bodies, dragons and cats decorated with deep streaks of red, blue, and golden glaze, and an extraordinary series of smooth, aerodynamic flying fish with complex patterns of dots along their glistening flanks. These works, along with his many paintings, sketches, and designs, made him famous. Before he died in 1961, he was awarded Japan's top accolade for artists, designation as a Living National Treasure.

By the time I emerged from Toki-no-Sato, the rain had stopped and I was eager to get back on the road. But before leaving, I took a path into the woods behind the museum to visit the Mano Mausoleum, last resting place of another famous exile who ended his days on Sado, the emperor Juntoku. Juntoku came to the throne in 1210, only twenty-five years after the Heian Period ended and effective power passed into the hands of military clans. The usurpers cared little for the Kyoto court and showed their disdain by setting up their capital in distant

Noh theater with outdoor stage

Kamakura to the east. Imperial resentment simmered quietly until 1219, when the sudden murder of the third Kamakura shogun encouraged the notion that things at the top were shaky; the incident was seen (rightly) as evidence of internal conflict among the dominant Hojo clan. Sensing their chance, nobles at the old court urged the emperor to take action and reclaim his authority.

What happened next came to be known by the splendid euphemism "The Jokyu Disturbance." After cogitating for two more years, Juntoku abdicated in favor of his infant son and dispatched an army to depose the regent in Kamakura. But the Hojo struck back hard, defeating the forces of the aristocratic party, confiscating their lands, and placing the imperial court under even stricter surveillance than before. The leaders of the revolt were sent into exile: Juntoku was shipped off to Sado, where he lived in the picturesquely named Palace of Unhewn Timber until he died twenty-two long years later. The stone mausoleum in which he is buried lies in a copse of tall cedar

Among the Exiles

trees and can be observed at a distance, from behind a fence, but not approached, even today.

Leaving history and culture behind, I walked away from the town of Mano and out onto the road along the coast of Ko-Sado. Clumps of wild lilies sprouting from the cliffside glowed orange in the bright sun, but the wind off the sea was chilly. Waves slammed into the rocks below, and dismal swathes of cloud swirled low over the mountaintops behind me. I remembered the warning of the old woman in the grocery and was glad I had decided to stick to the shore road.

Up ahead, the road was being widened and new tarmac laid by a work gang of both men and women. Trucks arrived one after another, depositing huge piles of fresh black gravel, which were then spread out with shovels and flattened with steamrollers. There was a clear and definite division of labor: men operated the machines, women did the shoveling.

Looking back at the sweep of Mano Bay and the tip of Nanaura Kaigan, now half-hidden in the afternoon haze, I reckoned I had covered a good eighteen miles during the day, perhaps more. My feet hurt and I needed a rest. But it seemed bad manners to lounge around in front of laborers sweating away to repair the road, so I forced myself to go on until I reached a narrow strip of stony beach below a tall cliff. I limped off the road and slumped thankfully down against a large rock. There was no one around and no sound except for the slow, rhythmic chattering noise made by the tumbling shingle as each receding wave dragged more of it down the slope.

An odd little "beep" above my head made me look up. It was the same unknown blue bird I had seen in Negai, a couple of days before. This time there were two of them: one was sitting above me on a telegraph wire while the other had flown higher up and was perched on a little ledge on the side of the cliff. The one on the wire, which I took to be the male, was watching his partner anxiously and chirping at her to come and join him. Evidently no soft touch, she wasn't taking any notice. Then, abruptly, she flew a little higher up and disappeared into some scrub growing out of the cliff. Occasional

109

SADO: JAPAN'S ISLAND IN EXILE

"beep beep" noises emerged, but nothing else. For a while the
male watched and waited, his eyes fixed on her hiding place . . .
and then suddenly out she came and he was off and following
her, up the cliff and out of sight.

A moment later, they were back. But now they had lost
each other. The male resumed his position on the wire, almost
exactly where he had been before, while the female was
perched on the same wire, a little further up. She was squeaking excitedly and had something in her beak, something that
looked like a worm. But the male wasn't taking any notice. This
didn't make sense. Okay, so this female evidently wasn't a
female, but another male, competing for her attention. Then I
spotted the original female again, fifty or sixty yards further
along the same telegraph wire; she was bobbing her tail and
beeping away in a sharp, clear little voice. But the two males
were now preoccupied with each other; they were edging cautiously along the wire, but in the wrong direction. And before
they could sort it all out, a heavy truck laden with stones rum-
bled round the corner a bit too fast and dropped a football-size
rock off the top of its load. It smashed as it hit the ground, and
the noise frightened all three of them away.

The stone-laden truck reminded me that I was in a part of
Sado long known for masonry. In the nineteenth century, there
were several actively worked quarries whose produce was
hauled laboriously over the hills to Ogi for export to the mainland. The area was also home to a renowned mason called
Gobei, maker of many roadside Jizos and a collection of eighty-
eight stone Buddhas that can still be seen at Iwaya Cave, near
Ogi. A little way ahead, if my calculations were correct, I would
come to a hamlet called Bentenmisaki where I could probably
get something to eat. The main road left the coast at that point
and turned inland, but according to the map there was a track
that followed the sea toward the big beach at Sobama where I
meant to camp for the night.

Bentenmisaki turned out to be a rocky little promontory
with a tiny shrine perched on top, high above the sea. The shrine
was made of sandstone and looked fantastically ancient, but the

110

Among the Exiles

ferocity of the rain, wind, and snow sweeping across the Japan Sea through the long winters could probably cause that much weathering in a dozen years. Inside the little shrine was a wooden tablet of the kind used to commemorate a departed ancestor. Usually such tablets are kept in the family home, so this one may have been made and deposited for the benefit of some nameless seaman who drowned here, far from wherever he came.

Below the promontory and facing out onto a small sandy beach was a cheerfully dilapidated inn with the mud-crusted remains of two abandoned swallows' nests stuck to the wall in the entrance-way. The owner, a middle-aged woman in a dark blue kimono and worn-out beach sandals and with a mouthful of startlingly gold teeth, greeted me deferentially. She would be glad to serve me a meal provided I didn't mind eating with all the other guests—she had a coachload of gateball players over from the mainland to take part in a competition and would be serving them all together in a little while. Gateball is a simplified form of croquet much beloved of senior citizens in Japan, so I had a good idea what my fellow diners would be like. Sure enough, as I sat there nursing a can of beer and looking out of the window at the sea, they began to emerge from their rooms, a group of old men of whom the youngest could not have been less than sixty-five, and a few looked well into their eighties. Despite their years, or perhaps because of them, and encouraged by the absence of their wives, they were behaving like unsupervised schoolboys, laughing loudly, pushing, showing off, and determined to make a night of it. They showed a polite interest in me, no more, as we took our seats at two long tables and tucked in to a prodigious meal of rice, soup, prawns, *buri*, squid and red snapper, buckwheat noodles with a hot mustard sauce, and sliced octopus on beds of dark, vinegar-flavored seaweed. A few of the more serious-minded gateballers were having a teetotal evening, fearful of spoiling their aim the next morning, but the majority were downing beer and sake as if tomorrow would never come. In between mouthfuls they cheerfully ragged each other, hiding a glass of beer when its owner was looking the other way, and picking out first this fel-

111

low, then that one, to make fun of. One timid little man, obviously the class wimp in his schooldays, sat nervously among them with rabbit teeth still protruding, eyes still blinking behind his glasses, still wanting to say funny things like the others but not quite daring, and being peremptorily sent, now by one, now by another, to fetch more rice or soup or beer from the sideboard. Laughter rang round the room, knees were slapped, spectacles were knocked askew, and snowy tufts of hair clinging precariously to the sides of balding scalps flopped into plates and wagged outrageously as the drink went down and the excitement mounted. I watched in fascination as one old fellow, his eyes dreamily focused on the mid-distance, slowly stuffed an enormous lettuce leaf into his mouth with his chopsticks, masticating each section in turn while the rest of the leaf drooped over his chin, for all the world like a giant tortoise.

By the time I was ready to pay up and leave the inn, it was almost dark. But the wind had dropped and the clouds had rolled away, so that there was enough light from the moon and stars for me to pick my way along the rough gravel track toward Sobama. The sea had quietened down too, and I could see the lights of several little boats already making their way out into the bay. My legs felt stiff and painful and I was just starting to wish I had asked for a room at the inn when I spotted an odd little structure down on the beach below the track. It was a primitive shelter for keeping a small boat, scooped out of a sand dune, a bit wider than a double bed and about twice as long. The sides were old pine posts driven deep into the sand, and there was a roof of rough thatch covered by an old net and weighted down with stones. Perfect. Too tired to bother with making a fire, I pushed my pack into the shelter, unrolled my sleeping bag, and crawled inside.

112

DAY 5

MUSIC THROUGH THE PINES

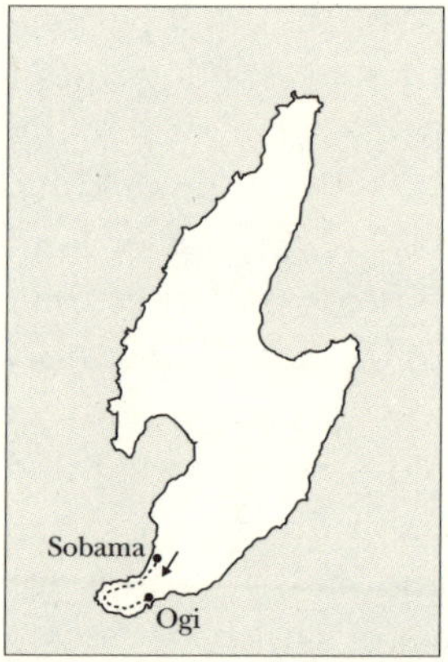

It rained in the night, but the next morning there were enough dry sticks under the eaves of my little shelter to get a fire going. The sky was completely covered by dull gray clouds except in the east, where dawn was cracking it open in thin streaks of pink, orange, and yellow. I made some tea and sat on the sand to drink it. Yellow speedwell, clover, and pink rockroses were growing in patches on the dunes, together with long, trailing arms of convolvulus that spread out in all directions and clambered over rocks, piles of driftwood, and even over the roof of the boat shelter, giving it the appearance of a neolithic cottage.

Below me, the beach was scattered with enormous quantities of garbage—torn nets draped over black rocks, huge broken chunks of polystyrene, battered plastic containers, contorted tree roots, lumps of smashed timber, cable drums, rusty iron pipes, squid lures, rubber shoes. Not much of it looked local. This was debris from ships, slung overboard some-

113

where at sea, thrown ashore by violent storms, dragged out into the bay again and then thrown back once more. Among the plastic bottles that still had legible labels were several with Korean or Russian writing.

My map showed a track running west behind the beach, but this had recently been upgraded to a proper tarmac road. Sobama has the biggest and best beach on the southern half of Sado, and plans were afoot to develop it. As well as a campground with its own bar-restaurant, someone had put up a brand new log house to provide tourist accommodation. A painted signboard hung outside, inscribed with the word "CULTOPIA." Many Japanese words are formed by bolting two or more concepts together, and the same principle had been applied to the concoction of this chilling hybrid. Culture and Utopia! When all you wanted was a room! Still, it wasn't particularly unusual. Japan coins new words like tokens spilling out of a one-armed bandit. In Sawada I had seen a car dealership whose name was "Heartpia," probably coined by the same klutz.

Beyond the western end of Sobama, every scrap of land was under the plough. There were some fields no larger than parking spaces, tidily planted with vegetables, and long tunnel greenhouses full of peppers and tomatoes. Here and there were orchards of fig, peach, and plum; old paint tins weighted with stones were hung from the branches of the trees to keep them growing low down. Most of the larger fields were used for tobacco, which was grown on raised rows of chocolate brown soil and then cut and hung to dry in long, low sheds of corrugated iron. In late summer, after the harvest, men and women can be seen in every village along this coast, sitting on wooden tubs in shed doorways, sorting the leaves into piles and then carefully stacking them in layers in tall barrels.

As the sun broke through the clouds, the sea swirled quietly round the black rocks and made dancing patches of purple, azure, and turquoise. Soon the early boats would be going out, including the circular tubs called *taraibune,* which the islanders use for collecting seaweed and shellfish from among the offshore rocks. Not many years ago there was enough and to spare

Music through the Pines

for everyone, but today the right to gather this valuable harvest is jealously guarded by the villagers who depend on it for a living: a fading monochrome poster pinned to the side of a wooden bus shelter portrayed a group of guilt-stricken young holiday-makers clustered round a string bag full of shellfish they had collected while a handsome, muscular young islander admonished them to keep their hands off other people's livelihoods.

In many places along this coast, huge, wide shelves of flat rock extend out into the sea, no more than a foot under water. The seaweeds that grow on them are easy to harvest in the sheltered bays, so the natural formations are copied by constructing huge, flat beds of concrete to serve the same purpose. Coming into the village of Etsumi, I found one of the natural ones, about three hundred yards long and extending about a hundred yards offshore. It was crowded with seagulls, thousands of them, white-bodied adults with yellow feet and slate gray wings, and youngsters with gray-brown baby plumage who struggled to stay upright as they practiced folding and unfolding their wings.

A pretty little shrine stood by the road in Etsumi, with two big old cherry trees, one on each side of the entrance, and an ancient stone column topped by a rough, moss-covered stone that looked like a mushroom cap. I stopped to give a tug on the red and white silk rope and say a short prayer. A group of three Jizo in knitted red caps watched impassively from their plinth on the left of the shrine and a large, glossy crow stared curiously down from the roof, its head cocked slightly to one side.

Outside, I was hailed by an old man who was squatting on his haunches beside the road. He wore a plum-colored anorak, black canvas shoes with no laces, and a long-peaked, war-vintage army cap. We talked for a few minutes about who I was and where I was going, and then he told me about his own travels, how he used to go away to find seasonal work in big cities like Tokyo, Osaka, and Nagoya, liked them well enough, made some money, but always came back home because "life is better in the place where you are born."

Across the road, the village harbor was busy with fisher-

115

SADO: JAPAN'S ISLAND IN EXILE

Unloading the catch at Etsumi

men getting ready to go out in their boats. The old man began talking about the *buri*, about regular catches of up to five thousand fish in a day, all weighing between eight and fifteen pounds, and the refrigerated trucks that came to pick them up and distribute them throughout Japan. With harvests of forty-five thousand pounds of fish a day, Etsumi ought to have been a wealthy place, but it certainly didn't look that way. Large catches were perhaps not quite as frequent as he wanted me to believe, and in any case were a brand new phenomenon. The fish, of course, had always been there, no doubt in even greater quantities, but no one would have bothered to even try and catch large numbers in the past because there was no distribution system through which to sell them.

"Are you going out to get *buri* this morning?" I asked him. The old man shrugged. "I don't know," he answered. This seemed a strange answer, but he rose to his feet, gestured for me to follow and walked over to where a group of younger men was stacking up empty fish boxes and sluicing off the boat

116

Music through the Pines

decks with pails of seawater. "You can come out with us if you want to," he told me. "Just wait until the boat is ready."

The sea lay in the harbor like glass, clear to the bottom and dappled here and there with rainbow colors where the men filling their tanks from plastic containers had accidentally splashed fuel into the water. Fish would be coming, and soon: I counted thirty-five kites on the harbor wall and about the same number on the telegraph wires overhead, all sitting still and bright-eyed with expectation. At a sign from the old man, I stepped aboard and took a place in the stern, out of the way. The engine coughed briefly, then started with a roar. We pulled away from the quay, swung round, and made for the open sea.

At barely twenty feet long, the boat was much smaller than the ones used by the fishermen of Washizaki. The fishing method was the same, but on a much smaller scale: the net was hauled in, and since the boat had no hold, the fish were dumped straight onto the deck. At first we landed only *iwashi* (sardines), squid, and mackerel. Some were trapped in the holes of the net, and if they couldn't easily be disentangled, the net was given a rough shake that sometimes cut the fish in half.

By the time we had hauled up the main net and tipped most of the contents on board, everyone was standing calf deep in fish. Most of them were little silver *aji*, or horse mackerel, but we also had several hundred sardines, some fat bream, a dozen snapper, some angel fish, a few flying fish, a black species called *mejina*, and another with silver stripes, called *shima-dai*, or "island bream." "Look here," called the old man, tossing yet another fish toward me. "That's the *inada* you were asking about." *Inada* is what *buri* are called when they are young, so I now understood his answer to the question I had asked him when we were first talking at the roadside: they were going out fishing, yes, but wouldn't know until they got there whether they would get any *buri* or not.

Less than an hour after setting off we were back on the quayside sorting out the catch. Someone drove up in a small truck laden with crushed ice, then pulled down the tailgate and shoveled the ice into a pile of shallow wooden boxes. We had about fifty large bream, two or three hundred steel blue mackerel, maybe five hundred sardines, and a few thousand of the small, low-value *aji*. First the larger fish were sorted by species, laid carefully in the boxes, nose to tail, covered with a sheet of blue plastic, and marked with the name of the Etsumi Fishing Cooperative. The humble *aji* didn't merit the same careful treatment: they were just pushed willy-nilly into the boxes that remained. Finally, each box was weighed, given another shovelful of ice, heaved up onto the back of another truck, lashed down with rope, and driven away. The whole job took less than an hour. It was an ordinary day.

I thanked the old man for letting me come out with them and indicated that it was now time for me to be getting on my way. He looked up in surprise. "What, without any breakfast?" he asked. While the others had taken care of the packing, he had been squatting on the quay in front of a wooden board laid on the top of an upturned bucket, cutting and filleting fish and throwing the offal into the sea, where the kites swooped down to recover it. "We eat after we finish work, you know," he told me, with a touch of severity. "Over there," he added, pointing toward a large concrete building behind me. "What's your hurry? You don't want to leave before breakfast, do you?"

The building was a two-story affair made of unpainted concrete blocks. Next to the main room, which was piled high with fishing gear, there was a smaller room containing a table and a dozen chairs, and leading off that, a kitchen. The table was covered with a sheet of checkered plastic, and on the wall above it hung a long banner inscribed with a prayer for large catches.

One by one, as they finished their tasks outside, the fishermen drifted in and joined the daily ritual of making their communal breakfast. To go with the rice, which had been cooking while we had been out in the boats and was now keeping warm in its electric pot, they prepared three enormous dishes—one each of raw squid, raw *buri*, and pickled radishes. From time to time, chunks of fresh mackerel and other fish were brought in

Music through the Pines

and added to a thick stew that was bubbling away in a heavy, smoke-blackened saucepan on the stove.

Everyone took part in these tasks except for one thin young man with a sharp, angular face, a mouthful of steel teeth, and shock of untidy black hair. His jobs were pouring everyone else's sake out into small glass tumblers and recording the morning's work in a ledger. As the others worked around him, he sprawled awkwardly over the table on his bony elbows, scratching his head doubtfully as he figured things out on scraps of paper. Having arrived at an answer, he would confirm it with the others before entering it carefully in the ledger. The talk of money was short and spare, conducted in monosyllabic grunts of which I understood little.

Just as we sat down to eat, the door flew open and another fisherman—not of our party, but dressed in the same thick green waterproof suit and rubber boots—burst into the room, calling out that he needed to use the phone. He was obviously upset—had his boat just sunk?—but whatever the problem was, no one felt the need to go out and investigate. Instead, they made a place for him at the table, urging him to sit down and eat. For a while he babbled on about his troubles, but the combination of sake and sympathy had its effect; soon he calmed down and even ventured a few sheepish grins.

Trying to understand their dialect was like cracking code. At first I could only catch two or three words out of a sentence, and had to guess the rest from the tone and gestures of the speaker. But as the meal progressed and the sake bottle circulated, my hosts got a better grasp of my ability and began to make allowances for it in the way they phrased their questions. There were many that they wanted to ask, driven partly by curiosity about the unfamiliar world from which I came, and partly by the wish to have their own dimly remembered impressions and certainties confirmed: that it rains in England more than in Japan, that the queen is a more visible figure than their own emperor, that London is regularly obliterated by pea-soup fogs, that English people always carry umbrellas, that English houses are bigger than those in Japan, that American English is

119

a variant of the British tongue and not vice versa. At the same time, they sought new information against which to compare their own circumstances: what did English people eat, what kinds of fish did they catch, how much money did fishermen earn, what kinds of boats did they use, and was it true that eldest sons did not always live with their aged parents, and if so, who cared for the old? Once the conversational ice had melted, they showed themselves much more inclined to talk and ask questions than their compatriot, the urban salaryman, whose repetitive routines and weighty corporate responsibilities effectively drain him of whatever natural curiosity he may ever have had.

By the time I had said my farewells and got back on the road, it was ten o'clock and I was drunk. Clumps of yellow rock lilies leaned out from the cliffs as though pointing, directing my attention to the sea. A dozen or so village women in wide-brimmed hats were drifting around the rocks offshore in their little circular *taraibune,* searching the seabed for *sazae* shells and seaweed. I watched them for a while in a stupor, then stumbled unsteadily down the road past long racks hung with ribbons of seaweed drying in the hot sun, coming eventually to the chunky whitewashed lighthouse at Sawasaki, the extreme southwest point of the island.

A footpath from the road to the lighthouse led across a headland with a couple of small fields where *yugao* were being grown—low, straggling plants with heavy, gourdlike fruits that lay on individual beds of straw on the ground. The base of each plant was carefully wrapped in its own straw jacket as well, to preserve it from cold, wet weather, and pests. Two old women were weeding the margins of the field side by side, hacking their way along the hedge with tiny sickles; they acknowledged my greeting with a wave, but without interrupting the rhythm of their work.

I sat on the edge of the headland and looked down at the shore. It was another chaos of jumbled chunks of lava, all pitted and gnawed and scooped out by the sea into shallow caves, long, narrow gullies, circular sink holes, and deep pools where

Music through the Pines

huge clumps of tawny orange weed heaved slowly up and down with the rise and fall of the incoming sea. Behind me was a grassy bank bordered by sweet-smelling rockroses; I leaned back and closed my eyes, lulled by the buzz of insects and the soft sloshing of the waves on the rocks below.

* * *

When I awoke, an hour later, the effect of my alcoholic breakfast had completely gone. It felt like the start of a new day. I shouldered the pack once more, took up Snake Frightener, and banged my way back onto the road leading away from the lighthouse. It climbed steeply up the hill above the village of Sawasaki, which lay at the head of a deep inlet with twenty or thirty small boats drawn up at the top of a wide concrete landing stage. A new coast road was under construction, so that in a year or two this old one would lose most of its traffic and revert to its original character as a quiet lane linking unvisited hamlets and isolated farms. The seaward side was edged with tiny fields, picked clean of weeds, while the mountain side had steep, lava-walled cliffs that had fallen away in some places to reveal layers of rich red earth lying on top of the volcanic rock. In some places the soil stratum was twenty feet deep or more, topped with a mass of tangled trees and shrubs that testified to its excellent fertility. No wonder this southern tip of Sado has yielded the best archaeological finds: the earliest inhabitants, no matter how primitive, would have gravitated here naturally,

Fisherman at Etsumi

SADO: JAPAN'S ISLAND IN EXILE

building their settlements where the farming was good, the weather benign, and the living easy.

The road climbed steadily upward, winding in tight loops first to the left, then to the right. Apart from birds and insects, there was no sound; no traffic passed in either direction, and when gaps in the hedge allowed a view of the surrounding fields, there was no one to be seen at work. At last I reached the crest of the hill and stopped to look back along the coast I had walked that morning. In the far distance I could see the inn where I had dined the night before and the long beach of Sobama where I had slept the night. But the village that had entertained me for breakfast was out of sight, tucked away beneath the cliffs.

Ahead, the road began its descent with a long, looping curve. A footpath plunged down into shady woods on my right, providing a shortcut across the loop, so I slithered down the steep embankment and followed it through the trees. The path was evidently little used; it was overgrown with grass, and every few yards I had to stop and brush huge spiderwebs aside with my hand. After a couple of minutes I emerged onto the road again, beside a small wayside statue of Jizo whose rough plinth of rock made a narrow ledge for two pale blue vases containing offerings of bright orange lilies. And while I was standing there looking at them, I heard a sound from somewhere down below the pines on the other side of the road—the slow, deep booming sound of a drum.

Percussion is generally agreed to have been the world's first form of instrumental music, and in Asia especially, drums have a long history of functions beyond simple entertainment. In ancient times, the territory of a Japanese village was defined by the area in which a drum beaten at an agreed spot was audible, and the sound of the drum was a signal used to call the inhabitants together. Even today the custom still survives in remote places (although most villages use a modern PA system), and every country festival features an element of *taiko*, in which both adults and youngsters take it in turns to pound large, deep-toned drums with short, thick, heavy drumsticks.

122

Music through the Pines

But a tiny wooden sign pointing down a track on the other side of the road told me that what I could hear was no festival practice. Carved in the sign was the single word, "Kodo."

The track descended steeply through the pine woods and emerged onto a patch of land that had been cut from the hillside into three flat terraces. On each level stood a building: at the far end was a modern structure, obviously residential; in the middle stood something that looked like a school assembly hall; and closest to where I was standing, with a rectangle of bare earth in front of it that was evidently destined to be a garden, was a curious black-and-white building that managed to look brand new yet venerable at the same time.

I walked over to it and peered in at the open door. There was a vestibule with a hard earthen floor where shoes were removed, a large, timber-floored hallway with a high ceiling supported by heavy black beams, and a wide wooden staircase at the back. A long rack with individual lockers for the shoes was fixed to the wall by the door, and on top of this lay an old stereo tape deck playing soft flute music. I called out a couple of times and waited, but no one came. When I stepped out into the sunshine again, I looked across the garden and there, halfway up an embankment on the far side, stood a small man in a large straw hat prising weeds out of the earth with a long-handled hoe. I called out again and this time he turned, leaning on his hoe like a staff and shading his eyes with his palm across his forehead.

I walked across to where he was standing. "Can I help you?" he asked.

"Well, yes," I said, "perhaps you can. I was just walking along the road up there when I heard something that . . . that sounded like a drum. So I came down the track there to see what it was."

The man looked at me with an air of quiet amusement. "Well, that's what it was," he replied. "A drum."

There was a pause.

"This is Kodo Village," he went on. "You knew that, of course. You saw the sign up by the road."

So much for my attempt to play the innocent traveler who had stumbled upon the place by accident. Kodo is famous and has no need of uninvited visitors. What would happen next would be another nosy intruder being sent brusquely on his way.

The man looked me up and down, taking in my dusty, unkempt appearance. "What are you doing on Sado?" he asked.

"Just walking," I told him. "Walking around the island."

"You look like you need a rest," he said, laying the hoe down on the ground. "Come inside for a while. I'll make us something to drink."

"I don't want to interrupt your work," I said.

"I know," he answered with a smile. "But I want you to. I feel like taking a break. I used to play the drums myself, but I retired last year. Takes it out of you, the drumming. So now I'm the gardener here. My name is Morita."

The inside of the building was dark and cool. Morita led me into a room with a brightly polished wooden floor and heavy beams in the walls and ceiling. He handed me a thin cushion to sit on and gestured to me to wait. After a few minutes he returned with a slim white coffeepot, two tiny cups, and a bowl of sweets, which he placed on the floor between us.

"What kind of house is this?" I asked him. "I've never seen one quite like it."

He laughed. "I'm not surprised," he said. "It's a rare sort of house. I don't even know if there's another one like it in Japan. It's an old Noh theater. We found it in Hamochi, a few miles from here. It was disused—there hadn't been a performance in it for years—so we bought it, took it to pieces, brought it here by truck, and reassembled it. Took a long time. Just to set up the basic structure took nearly a month. Look how heavy the beams are! If we'd known how much work it would be, we would probably never have started."

He poured the coffee out into the little cups and pushed one over to me. And then, because he knew I wanted to know, he told me about Kodo.

124

Music through the Pines

The seeds of this remarkable musical community were sown some twenty-five years ago, when the youth of Japan was gripped by the spirit of the 1960s. It was a time of social and political ferment: there were demonstrations against the continuing American occupation of Okinawa, more demonstrations against the Vietnam War, and a general atmosphere of protest against the growing national obsession with material success. Art, theater, film, and literature all provided fertile ground for trying out the new theories of alternative culture, and oddball social experiments were sprouting up all over the country like toadstools.

In 1970, an entrepreneur called Tagayasu Den came up with the idea of conducting a summer music school on Sado. As well as attracting musicians, he hoped it would generate interest in the island itself—perhaps create some work for a few of the islanders and help to stem the steady flow of youngsters leaving to look for jobs on the mainland. Fifty or so people took part in the summer school, and by the time it was over, a core group of about a dozen young men had made up their minds to stay on Sado and set up a permanent community. They planned to live a spartan, frugal existence and devote themselves to studying the ancient art of the drum. Ondekoza was the name they chose for their group, *ondeka* being island dialect for "Demon Drum."

Taking up residence in a former school building, the community embarked on a lifestyle that was as spartan as any of them could have wanted, and then some. At twenty years older than the others, Den was the natural leader, and the regime he established was strict. Tobacco, alcohol, and personal relationships with the opposite sex were all banned. So was personal money; any assets belonging to group members were pooled. And on top of the rigorous program of musical study, there was plenty of physical exercise, including long cross-country runs before breakfast every morning.

While other experimental communes bloomed and then quickly withered all over Japan, Ondekoza hung in there and survived. Despite its nonmaterialist principles, some income

125

was necessary, and Den devised various schemes to obtain it, including pestering big companies to support the revival of "traditional" Japanese music. This idea met with approval in conservative boardrooms, but aroused suspicions elsewhere. People speculated about the group's true motives. Were they emperor-worshiping rightist fanatics? Dangerous left-wingers plotting a revolution? Adherents of some bizarre religious sect?

The truth was much more simple. Ondekoza's religion was wholly focused on the drum, and the ascetic way of life was adopted for no more sinister purpose than to hone minds and bodies in the service of performance. As time went by and their skills grew, they studied other musical forms, instruments, and dances, and assimilated them into their repertoire.

The natural development of the group should have been a growth in confidence and maturity, and a parallel relaxation of the stern daily discipline. But if this was what they wanted, it was the opposite of what they got. Den's role as leader made him increasingly autocratic. He also invested their meager earnings from performances in a series of unsuccessful films. By 1981, the others had had enough. There was a series of painful confrontations leading up to a final break. Den departed in a huff, taking both the drums and the name with him. The remaining members recast their community in a more democratic form and adopted a new name—Kodo, which means "heartbeat."

Morita reached for the coffeepot and refilled our little cups.

"I guess I was lucky," he said. "By the time I arrived here, Den had already left. It was winter. I was camping out by myself on the beach near Mano. That's where I met the group—they used to come down to the beach to run. We talked, and I decided to join them. It was hard at first. The financial problems hadn't been sorted out, and the group was working to get hold of new equipment. Once we'd done that, things got easier."

This seemed a very modest way of putting it. What happened in fact was that Den's traumatic departure unlocked precisely the blend of community spirit, dedicated profes-

Music through the Pines

sionalism, and musical excellence that he himself had wanted to build. The new group made its debut at the 1981 Berlin Festival and went on to perform before packed houses in Japan and overseas—New York, London, Paris, Madrid, Rio. Today, having given something like two thousand concerts in thirty different countries, Kodo has become Japan's most widely traveled and acclaimed musical ensemble, with an international reputation that sells thousands of recordings and brings invitations from any and all of the world's most prestigious concert halls.

"Nowadays, we're on the road a lot of the time," said Morita, "but we're always here at the end of August, for the Earth Celebration. You ought to come along. It's not just Kodo. Groups and performers come from all over the place—Africa, Indonesia, the Philippines, Puerto Rico. It's all about learning new styles, trying new ideas, mixing instruments, exploring the whole world of percussive music. I'll show you."

He rose and left the room, returning quickly with a brochure about the previous year's festival. On the front cover was a poem, written in Japanese and English. The title was "Roads across the Sea."

> *Dreaming of lands beyond the line where sea meets sky*
> *We load our ships with the rhythms of our home*
> *To trade with people who dance to different tunes*
> *Listen to our dreams, help us build these bridges.*

"It's quite a party," he went on. "More and more people come every year. Including, nowadays, local dignitaries—town councilors and so on. Quite a change from the old days. So we're always here on Sado at the end of August. And we always come back to spend the winter here, too. Up until a couple of years ago, we were based in an old school, a few miles from here. But we needed more room, so in the end we bought this bit of land to live on, have a purpose-built place to practice and try to be self-supporting." He chuckled quietly. "Not as easy as it sounds, though. The land looks fertile enough, all covered with trees and bushes, but cultivating it is another story. It's completely virgin, you see—never been used for anything. No natural fertilizer, no worms, not even much water. We don't use any artificial fertilizer, so the only way to get it going is by natural crop rotation, using the crops that people on Sado have always grown—clover, barley, things like that. It's a slow process. Come on outside, I'll show you round."

We went out into the sun again, and I followed him up a narrow footpath that he himself had cut into the forest. There were a few cedars and several thick clumps of tall, powdery green bamboo, but most of the trees were deciduous, growing out of a rich, deep bed of ancient leafmold. "I'm a complete beginner at all this," Morita admitted. "Don't know the names of most of the plants, and tend to forget a lot of the ones I learn. But I'm getting better, little by little. This one, for instance," he bent down, indicating a low, spreading plant with leaves like a nasturtium, "is called *fuki*. If you boil the stalks and peel them, you can eat them as a vegetable. And that tree there, with those hard gray spikes sticking out of the trunk, is *tara-no-ki*—be careful you don't touch it. And then there's this shrub here. It's called . . ." He screwed up his face and scratched his head. "Can't remember. But pick a few of the leaves and rub them between your fingers." The leaves were tiny and fleshy; they left a yellow smear on my fingers that smelled of lemon. "Good for cooking," said Morita.

Were there any animals in the forest? "Not many," he said. "Fewer than I expected, anyway. There are *tanuki*, of course, and weasels, and rabbits. And a few snakes. But no monkeys—at least, I've never seen one. And no foxes, either. They say that there have never been foxes on Sado."

Morita's path described a wide circle through the trees and came out at the top of an embankment overlooking Kodo Village. We slithered down and walked across his garden. Here and there, thin seedlings of clover were struggling to establish themselves, but most of the cleared land was bare, hard-packed earth, sandy orange in color. It looked to me as if Morita was pecking at the problem. The whole place needed to be prop-

128

Music through the Pines

erly ploughed before there would be any chance of raising decent crops.

Adjoining the garden was a yard with a couple of battered pickup trucks and three trail bikes parked together. A bare-chested man with a long ponytail was building a line of wooden steps from one edge of the yard down to the door of a long, two-story building—"the residential block," said Morita. There were two other buildings as well, one of which served as an office. The other was the group's practice hall. Morita pushed open one of the tall wooden doors and gestured to me to follow.

Inside, the hall looked like a cross between a gymnasium and a church. From the tops of heavy timber pillars against the walls rose multilayered glulam beams that curved up to form a row of five giant arches supporting the ceiling. The beams, floor, and walls were all made of some light-colored wood, evenly grained and smoothly varnished, and the windows were flanked by long, heavy curtains of dark blue velvet. All around, neatly stacked in readiness for the next session, were the tools of the group's percussive trade.

At the back, mounted on heavy black frames with solid wooden wheels, stood the two colossal *o-daiko,* or "great drums," each hewn from the trunk of a mighty zelkova tree and covered at each end by the hide of a whole cow. Their awesome size gave them the otherworldly aspect of sacred clan totems and a sound to match—a thunderous, bone-quivering boom like the pulse of the cosmos itself.

At a suitably respectful distance, junior members of the arsenal were stacked along the walls like military subordinates: fat, shiny brown *chu-daiko* (middle drums); matte black *o-kedo* (marching drums), built of separate staves bound tightly together to give a lighter, sharper sound; and the smaller *shime-daiko* (tie-up drums), whose skin tension is adjustable and has to be tightened each time the drums are used. To demonstrate what this involved, Morita picked one off the top of the stack and sat on the floor, gripping it with his feet and hauling on the thick ropes while an imaginary partner pounded them into submission with a heavy club.

129

"It was wonderful, playing the drums," said Morita when we stepped outside. "You can't compare it with anything, the way it takes you over, body and soul. But it's harder work than anything I'd ever done before. I still play now and again, informally, but I couldn't manage it full-time anymore. Arthritis," he added with a grimace, pointing to his knees, "or something like that. But I like messing about in the garden, working at my own pace. And my place is nearby—just a few minutes' walk away."

"You don't live here?"

"No, I moved out when I stopped playing. Rented a little house in a village down the road. Three rooms with a balcony on the top floor, overlooking the sea. It's quiet, of course—too quiet for some, I suppose. But I like it. And it doesn't cost much."

"Could you find a place to buy if you wanted to?" I asked him. "Are houses cheap here?"

He laughed. "Well yes, they're cheap enough. Very cheap, in fact. The problem about buying a place isn't the money. It's that people who own property don't want to sell it. All these new roads being built, and new harbors—it makes the islanders think that prosperity is coming. Crazy to sell in that situation. And although locals can find a place to buy easily enough—a young couple getting married, for instance—it's not the same for outsiders. I mean people from the mainland wouldn't get anything. At least, not until everyone in the village agreed. And that could take years. I daresay I could buy a place in a year or two—that's to say if I had the money, and if I really wanted to. But I don't."

There was a moment's silence, a moment in which Morita looked at me with his head bent slightly to one side and a quizzical look of enquiry on his face, as if to ask if there was anything else I wanted to know. Then he took Snake Frightener from where I had left it, leaning against the wall of the rehearsal hall, and handed it to me.

"Here you are, pilgrim," he said with a grin. "Don't forget this. You'll be going on to Ogi now." It was a gentle dismissal, not a question. "Used to be the most important town

Music through the Pines

on Sado, Ogi did. In the old days, I mean. Because it's the only place with a really good natural harbor. And that made it the main port in every other way, too—bars, flophouses, gambling, girls . . . everything. Lots of trade—not just gold from the old mine, but everything else as well. Not any more, of course. Nowadays Sawada is the administrative capital. Mano has most of the hotels, most of the tourists, and I suppose Ryotsu would be the principal town, the 'biggest' town, because it's the main ferry port. Funny thing, though—Ogi still has more life, more action, than any of them. Late at night, it's the only place on the island with anything happening."

I shouldered my pack, thanked him for showing me round, and shook his hand. Then we each took a pace back and bowed to each other. "Send me a postcard sometime," he said. I turned away and set off up the track through the pine trees to the road on the ridge above us.

* * *

A couple of hundred yards ahead, the road swung to the left, but there was a narrow path that went straight ahead, directly toward the sea, signposted to a place called Inukamidaira. I followed its steep downward slope, between clumps of blue hyacinth and wild strawberry just coming into fruit, until it emerged into a tiny, sheltered bay with a wide, curving wall of pitted lava on one side. Below this wall was a broad ledge of rock where an old fisherman in a grubby singlet and khaki shorts was patiently untangling a large, russet-colored net and hanging it up on a bamboo frame. On the other side of the bay were three tiny paddies planted with young green shoots of rice. One of the paddies had eight kites standing around its edge, obviously waiting for a frog to show itself: they stood stock still, deep in concentration, as brown and sinister as a bunch of Chicago hit men in raincoats, waiting for their target to come out of a restaurant. They ignored me as I passed quietly by on the path, which wound this way and that among the rocks for a short way and then climbed back up the cliff and back onto the road, a little way short of a brand-new bridge marked with a sign that said "Shiomibashi."

131

SADO: JAPAN'S ISLAND IN EXILE

The bridge spanned a pretty little bay formed by the curve of craggy lava cliffs topped with grass, wild flowers, and a few stunted pines. At the far end, a flight of concrete steps led down to a narrow, stony beach and a patch of glassy-smooth sea decorated by three or four tiny islets. I ran down the steps, threw my clothes in a heap on the shingle, and plunged into the water. It was cold and clear, falling away to deep chasms between the islets. Every rock was studded with shells, and when I dived to examine them I startled a fat brown octopus from its hole beneath a ledge; it wriggled away and moved briskly off with strong, pumping strokes of its muscular body, trailing long tentacles in its wake.

The old port of Ogi, where I planned to stop for the night, was now only a few miles distant—near enough to be in sight if not for the intervening cliffs and headlands. Rather than climb back up to the bridge, I continued along the shore, clambering over rocks and jumping over inlets, crossing the widest by means of a heavy log jammed across it like a bridge. The rocks here were pure lava, as sharp and gritty as compacted cinders, and eroded into the most fantastic shapes I had seen anywhere on the island so far. Two or three times I stopped in amazement at what looked like prehistoric relief carvings with hieroglyphic captions on distant patches of cliffside; but each time I approached them they turned out to be natural formations, jumbles of bumps, gullies, and crevices chiseled out of faults in the rock by storm-flung waves and tearing winter winds. Here and there at my feet were fissures and sinkholes, some as small as teacups, where enough soil had collected to sustain anemones, asters, and a new, southern species of lily with short, tough, leafy stems and a speckled, reddish orange flower. Eventually the shore widened out into a broad ledge where old lava flows had run down to the sea and been frozen in their original form by sudden contact with the cold water, leaving successions of low, stony, jagged-edged wavelets as bare and dusty as the surface of the moon. This ledge continued round the base of the cliff into a small bay and rejoined the road from Shiomibashi bridge at the little village of Shukunegi.

132

Music through the Pines

Women fishing,
and taraibune

Even by Sado's standards, Shukunegi is a relic from another era. Once renowned as a shipbuilding center, it's now more like a ghost town, still and silent, with old wooden houses packed together along streets too narrow for any vehicle wider than a bicycle. Some are deep gullies covered by slabs of stone with streams gurgling beneath them, others no more than alleys cobbled with smooth boulders and bordered by chilly patches of deep green moss. The houses are ramshackle, of unpainted timber split by the weather, with ill-fitting doors, cracked window shutters, and walls that lean inward or outward at alarming angles. The single modern building is a combined general-store-and-post-office beside the road; I called in to buy a can of beer and sat to drink it on the only patch of open ground I could find, a small grassy spot outside a temple. A sign in front announced the presence of a statue of the goddess Kannon, made by the mason Gobei, and the grave of Shuzo Shibata, a famous local cartographer.

There was no one around except a large black-and-white cat sitting on the bridge in the sunshine licking an extended hind leg. After a few minutes, two elderly women carrying battered straw baskets shuffled quietly past me but didn't look in my direction. The absence of modern development in the village is deliberate, and the studied indifference to strangers likewise; yet despite its neglected appearance, Shukunegi is more than accustomed to the attentions of outsiders. Like

133

SADO: JAPAN'S ISLAND IN EXILE

other out-of-the-way places on Sado, it is often used by television companies in need of old-fashioned locations for shooting period dramas, and although this brings welcome revenue, it also brings coachloads of eager fans who want to stop, explore, and photograph the actual spots (some even marked with plaques) where they have seen innocent maidens pursued and kidnapped, and top-knotted villains cut down by the flashing swords of samurai heroes.

Just outside the village I came to a long, low wooden building that looked like a schoolhouse, with a painted signboard inscribed with the words "Sado Folklore Museum." An old man with round glasses perched on the end of his nose sold me a ticket and waved me inside to explore. There were no signs for visitors and no coherent attempt to sort things into categories: the exhibits were simply crammed together in a succession of dusty, cavernous rooms. Like many provincial museums, and not only in Japan, this one contained a handful of valuable and interesting items mixed up with large quantities of junk. One room offered a display of daily work-tools: mattocks, harrows, winnowing baskets, huge black-toothed logging saws, battered old lanterns crusted with rust, and several long tridents for fishing. An old sepia photograph pinned to the wall showed half a dozen women brandishing these instruments as they waded up to their waists in the sea, while in the background, others were shown collecting seaweed, apparently scratching it off rocks with fingers curved like claws.

The next room contained several elaborately made wooden chests with tiny drawers, two large looms, and, without any obvious connection, a vivid display of paintings that illustrated the horrors of hell. One showed half a dozen monstrous snakes, grinning with hideous delight at the sight of people being dropped upside down into a deep pit; another pictured screaming victims being boiled alive in cauldrons of hot oil. Elsewhere, sinners were shown being pounded flat by demons with huge hammers, others staked out and sizzling away on red-hot grills, and still others being chased naked through a forest of spiky trees by ferocious, fire-breathing dogs. One unfortu-

134

Music through the Pines

nate, chained to a tree, was having his guts slowly extracted by a horned figure with a pair of giant pliers, another was being carefully chopped into small pieces by a goblin with an axe, and a final group, some of whom looked remarkably like members of the incumbent government, were being slowly squashed between two enormous flat rocks by a pair of laughing demons.

Immediately adjacent to this bloodthirsty display was a collection of shrine paraphernalia: old images of Buddha, their paint cracked and chipped, some ceramic bells, a few battered drums, eleven candlesticks still crusted with wax, and, curiously, two beautifully carved wooden penises, considerably larger than life, and two wooden forearms with closed fists of exactly the same dimensions. That the penises were fertility-cult objects I could easily accept, but the forearms had me baffled. In the absence of explanation, instruments of masturbation, real or symbolic, was the best guess I could make. If I was right, then local standards of decency were perverse: on the wall above were several old photographs of islanders at work, yet the old custom of women working bare-breasted out of doors, which was still normal practice on Sado up to World War II, was not shown—vetoed, perhaps, by some modern-minded functionary who considered the idea improper.

Outside in the afternoon sunshine, the road to Ogi swung round in a long curve through neat paddies where young rice plants stood in gleaming rectangles of water as still and orderly as companies of soldiers on parade. At a track that led off to the left, a signpost proposed a short diversion to Iwaya Cave, the other end of the trans-Sado tunnel supposedly excavated by the miracle-working priest Kobo Daishi; the other end, at Iwayaguchi, was the cave where I had stopped on the second day of my journey and seen the mysterious broken-necked doll seated by the edge of a dark pool of water. The distance between the two caves was nearly the length of the whole island, so it seemed worthwhile to stop off and see what kind of terminus Kobo Daishi had supplied at this end of his masterwork.

The path climbed steeply through a thick forest and came

135

SADO: JAPAN'S ISLAND IN EXILE

Hut by the sea near Ogi

out on an open area of grass with Gobei the mason's eighty-eight stone Buddhas ranged round its edge in a semicircle. The cave was a tall crack in the cliff opening into a high-ceilinged chamber with shelves cut into the stone walls and crammed with hundreds of Jizo figures. I examined them as best I could in the dim light and noticed that they were all slightly different; perched together on their stone ledges, with heads inclined this way and that, some with their hands folded in their laps and others with a hand or arm upraised, they looked for all the world like a gathering of ancient ecclesiastics who had come to the cave for a conference and been turned to stone in the midst of their discussions. As at Iwayaguchi, the depths of the cave were in complete darkness, making it impossible to tell how far it extended.

Another path led off into the forest from near the mouth of the cave, heading back toward the road but signposted to "Shiawase Jizo." This turned out to be an enormous statue, some twenty-five feet high, that stood on a plinth at the top of a

136

Music through the Pines

steeply sloping enclosure. Being recently made, it still had a hard-edged, machine-finished look, but a few seasons of exposure to Sado's weather would soon give it the patina of age appropriate to its position and significance.

Just what that significance might be was hard to guess; apart from the main statue, the compound contained a number of tiny huts, shaped like shrines, surrounded by hundreds of Jizo figures and also penis-and-testicles talismans. Made to a consistent pattern, the penises were short and chubby, pointing upward at a slight angle to the vertical, like missiles ready for launching, and resting on bases formed by the two balls. Some even had little faces carved between the balls, which stared back at me with cheerful grins when I bent to examine them. One of the shrines appeared to be dedicated to the local *tengu;* as well as the standard masks there was a beautiful old head of the original member of the species, the birdlike *karasu-tengu,* with holes for the eyes, two sharply pointed little ears, and a good, strong, flesh-tearing beak. By chance or design, the same altar was also furnished with several more of the now-familiar penis emblems, including one magnificent specimen carved from some dark hardwood, about three inches in diameter, with every knotty vein in the stalk and every fold of skin at the base of the helmet carefully, even lovingly, defined. At the bottom of the hill stood a wooden shack that contained the shrine shop, but it was closed; peering through the window I could see racks of postcards, pens, dolls, and key rings dangling white or black plastic versions of male genitalia to the standard design. Before the war, shrines like this where women could pray for a successful pregnancy were common all over Japan, but today they are seen less often. Still, if this one was typical of the enthusiasm with which fertility was usually invoked, the power of suggestion must surely have had some effect. With interestingly erect penises in such profusion, many of the supplicants must hardly have been able to wait until they got home.

The sun hung low in the sky, spreading red and peach-colored streaks through the clouds on the horizon, as I turned the last corner on the plateau above Ogi and started down the hill

137

SADO: JAPAN'S ISLAND IN EXILE

into the town. Coming the other way was a young teenage boy in his black school uniform, pushing a bicycle with one hand and concentrating deeply on a magazine held in the other. He passed by without noticing my presence, but close enough for me to see what he was reading so intently; it was a full-page cartoon depicting a schoolgirl, her uniform torn in shreds from her body, spreadeagled on a table, and being ingeniously violated by four or five blue-jawed psychopaths at the same time.

From the top of the hill, Ogi's suitability as a port was immediately obvious. A great arc of cliff lay round the south side of the harbor, like an encircling arm protecting it from the weather, and the sea in the bay lay smooth and still with opalescent patches glinting on the surface. The shore here continues flat, or gently sloping, well back from the sea, and the town gives the impression of being built on just the right scale: not cramped and poky like Shukunegi, nor dank and gloomy like gold-mining Aikawa, nor with the sprawling, unplanned, municipal-bus-station look of Sawada, but with streets of a sensible width and plenty of open spaces. On a bluff overlooking the sea is a large park with shady walks along tree-lined pathways surrounding an area of open grass—the site of Kodo's annual Earth Celebration—and at the foot of the same hill stands Kisaki Shrine, a beautifully proportioned building roofed with curving, reddish brown tiles, decorated with ceramic chrysanthemums, and flanked by two stone lanterns half-covered by gray-green lichens.

Despite occasional signs of halfhearted repair and refurbishment, the buildings along Ogi's main street were recognizably made in the old Echigo style, using heavy wooden boards for the walls and thick wooden shingles weighted with stones for the roof. The older shops occupied the front rooms of long, slim houses built at right angles to the street and with the kitchen and living area at the back, reached by a narrow, dirt-floor passage. Stopping off at a grocery store where oranges, cabbages, pumpkins, bananas, and fat shoots of young bamboo were displayed in boxes on the street, I went inside and called out to the owner; a few moments later she hobbled out along

138

Music through the Pines

her dark, low passage, sold me a couple of oranges, and gave me directions to a little inn down by the port. I found it next door to a souvenir shop. The rate was cheap, and cheaper still if I didn't want a meal provided.

After a long soak in the bath and a couple of beers, I went out again to explore the town. Although I had covered less distance this day than on any other so far, I must have been more tired than I realized: no coherent memory of the evening remains but only a succession of fragments—a plate of fried *gyoza* dumplings in one place; a sake-drinking session in another; some deep red slices of tuna on a long, oval dish with scalloped edges; beer in a dingy, smoke-filled den where men with rags round their heads were shouting at each other; and somewhere, connected to nothing in particular, an enormous porcupine fish, stuffed and mounted in a display case, staring into the distant distance, as if dreaming of the sea, with a single bulbous, green glass eye.

DAY 6

SHIP
HORSE
PICTURE

Right in front of Ogi port there's a large open plaza, and in the middle of the plaza there's a museum, and upstairs in the museum, occupying a wall thirty feet long, there's a map that illustrates the sailing and trading routes used in medieval times along the whole coast of the Japan Sea. From Hokkaido in the north to Shimonoseki in the far southwest, sixty-one separate ports are shown, plus Ogi itself, the only sizable link in the chain that is not sited on the mainland.

What's immediately obvious, given Japan's rugged geography and limited system of roads, is that most goods and passengers with any distance to travel had to be moved by sea. The map shows half a dozen regular, direct routes between Sado and the mainland (compared with only three today), but Ogi was evidently an important stop-off port for a lot of the long-distance traffic as well: ships calling in to discharge or take on part of a load, to replenish supplies, and to seek shelter from bad weather. A display board in the museum claims that Ogi harbor

140

Ship Horse Picture

could accommodate as many as five hundred ships at one time, and often did so—all of them, of course, with harbor dues to pay. Five hundred may be an exaggeration—certainly it seems a fantastic number today—and it's not at all clear what kinds or sizes of vessels were counted as "ships" in order to arrive at such a total. But from the early seventeenth century, when gold from the Kinzan mine was shipped to the mainland from Ogi, and probably for centuries before that, the town must have enjoyed a level of prosperity and importance vastly out of proportion to the relative poverty of the island as a whole. Provincial Japanese ports in medieval times had plenty of opportunities to grow rich as the quantity and variety of trading goods increased and as local outbreaks of civil war made them useful as bases of military supply. Construction flourished, especially of premises concerned directly or indirectly with distribution—warehouses, wholesalers, inns, and pawnbrokers—and, if trade was sufficient, commercial guilds were established to protect the interests of merchants specializing in particular categories of goods, from hats and furniture to fish and salted vegetables. As well as carpenters, shipwrights, and greengrocers, even a place like Ogi would have had its pharmacists, hairdressers, tailors, dyers, and drapers, as well as separate dealers for products like oil, soy sauce, vinegar, rice, fertilizer, and fancy goods. Today, only the faintest traces of all this bustling enterprise remain. Sado has reverted to its natural status as a commercial backwater, and a first experience of Ogi's slow, subdued atmosphere, dusty streets, dilapidated buildings, and general air of benign neglect makes it hard to imagine that the past was ever any different.

The standard coaster that plied between Ogi and the mainland was a tough, solidly built little vessel about sixty feet long, with three masts, of which the tallest, in the middle, was about the size of a modern telegraph pole. All three were rigged with sails kept taut by bamboo rods inserted through loops or sleeves, which also allowed them to be easily turned this way and that. There was no shelter on deck beyond a simple awning: the helmsman stood in the stern, steering by means of a heavy wooden tiller slotted into the top of the rudder and altering course in response to shouted commands from a navigator in the bow. A large hatch in the deck gave access to a capacious hold in which to carry the island's exports: bamboo, clay tiles, stoneware, bundles of firewood, straw sacks of rice and seaweed, jars of miso paste and sake, pottery, tools, articles of furniture, and quantities of dried fish.

Longer journeys required more substantial ships, and these were built with a high, curving prow and a raised stern section incorporating a large cabin with "windows" of heavy latticework. Here the crew could cook meals and boil water for tea in a kettle suspended from the galley ceiling. The captain's own cabin was built inside the first; here he could keep his chests, books, writing materials, and navigation instruments. Ships of this type can be seen in several pictures hung inside Ogi's Kisaki Shrine, all painted on wooden tablets and all to the same formula. Making its way from right to left across a mauvy blue sea, with the mountains of Sado in the background and the sun rising behind them, the ship is shown in full sail, with the crew on deck all facing toward the bow and the captain alone in the raised stern, also facing forward and apparently shouting orders. These paintings were not made for amusement, nor for art's sake; they were votive pictures, called *funaema* (literally "ship horse pictures"). A separate painting was commissioned for each ship and stored in a temple in its home port. There it stayed, an iconographic representation of the "soul" of the ship and its crew, which could be directly addressed when praying for their protection or preserved as a memento in the event of their loss at sea. Dependent since earliest times on fishing, the people of Sado have always been devout worshipers of sea deities, forever praying for calm seas and big catches. Even today, no one rescued from some peril of the sea would fail to go straight to a sea god's shrine to give thanks and make as generous an offering as he could afford.

Despite the excesses of the night before—or whatever it was that happened—I was lacing up my boots by the inn's front door soon after five o'clock the next morning. Even that wasn't too

Ship Horse Picture

early for my hostess, who shuffled out in her carpet slippers to bid me farewell and ask where I was headed. "Akadomari," I told her, mentioning the name of the next substantial port up the coast, and she brought her hands together in a gesture of pleased anticipation. "Oh yes, Akadomari," she repeated with a smile. "Well that's a nice walk for you. The coast is really beautiful."

In truth, the coast road north from Ogi is not "really beautiful" at all, but singularly monotonous, which was why I had already made my mind up to leave it at Hamochi, the next village, and make a looping detour to Akadomari through the hills. "Are you sure you know the way?" the old lady asked anxiously when I explained this modified plan. "Do be careful now—make sure you don't get lost. People do get lost in the mountains, you know. I'm afraid to go up there, haven't been for . . . why, twenty years or more. It's better down here, close to the sea."

A thin mist hung over the sea as I walked down to the harbor and then out of Ogi along the road to Hamochi. On the landward side was a low, crumbling cliff and on the other a smooth expanse of water where a couple of rust-streaked trawlers and the last stragglers from Ogi's squid-fishing fleet could be seen making their way back to port. Now that I had rounded the southern corner of the island I was back on the Uchikaifu coast; and like the northern section where my journey had begun, this southern part consisted of long, narrow rock-strewn beaches separated from each other by stubby, semi-accessible headlands and marked off from the road by a thick concrete seawall. But away to the left I could see the low, green foothills of Ko-Sado bathed in the early morning light, and I pressed on eagerly to the junction at the mouth of the Hamo River. Here I could turn away from the coast and cross the patchwork of rice fields leading to the village of Hamochi and the wooded hills beyond.

After Kuninaka, Sado's central plain, the south-facing Hamochi lowlands rank second in rice production and, thanks to plentiful fresh water from the river and higher average temperatures than anywhere else on the island, provide the highest

143

Kisaki Shrine, Ogi

yield per acre as well. Before the war there were two big miso factories here as well, each employing around two hundred people and producing upwards of six hundred tons a year. But supplying the ingredients for such large-scale enterprises was far beyond the capacity of the impoverished local farmers: the soybeans and even the salt were imported from the mainland, and virtually all the finished miso exported right back again. The reason for conducting the operation on Sado was simply that the islanders' labor was cheap—around seventy-five sen a day, compared to a whole yen or more elsewhere. The business folded in Japan's postwar economic chaos, leaving rice as the end of Hamochi's prosperity as well as its beginning; but today, with support from big food companies like Marudai, local miso is making a comeback.

Despite the early hour, a few old women were already at work in Hamochi's fields, bending double to thin out the young rice shoots by hand or moving as lightly as birds along the narrow, grassy embankments dividing the paddies. The village itself was deserted: I stopped to buy a can of iced coffee from a machine and sat to drink it with no one for company

Ship Horse Picture

but one of the life-size plastic policemen that local forces set up along country roads throughout Japan to remind motorists to observe the speed limit. Between us in the road, flattened from end to end by a passing truck, lay a long brown snake with black zigzags along its back. I examined the snake and the policeman examined me, while from a doorway up the street a sad-eyed and very elderly beagle swung its head slowly from side to side, examining both of us.

Beyond the village, the road rejoined the bank of the river and wound along to a fenced-in enclosure with a large sign marked "Sado Botanical Gardens" above its firmly locked gate. Next door, shaded by a grove of tall trees, was a temple where preparations were evidently being made for some ceremony. Here and there in the graveled forecourt were a huge stack of sake barrels wrapped in straw, a large drum, a heap of lion-dance masks and costumes, the front half of a wooden horse, several flags and banners, and a pair of long bamboo poles linked by strings from which hundreds of twisted papers, each one inscribed with a prayer, dangled like so much washing hung out to dry. I wondered what kind of occasion these objects had been set out for—a performance of *tsuburosashi,* perhaps. This ancient ritual is supposed to have originated in Hamochi and is still danced from time to time at some of the village shrines. *Tsuburo* is a large, cucumber-shaped vegetable, and the meaning of *sashi* is "to penetrate." The male dancer, his face concealed by a mask, lumbers about holding the base of a long wooden phallus to his groin with one hand and rubbing it lasciviously with the other, while his two female partners, representing a pair of goddesses called "Shagiri" and "Zeni Daiko," skip nimbly this way and that just out of his reach. Another possibility was a rehearsal of *harukoma* (or, as the island dialect has it, *harigoma*) in which the celebrants set off round the village carrying a wooden horse *(koma)* on their shoulders and dance from house to house collecting money or offerings for the shrine. The principal dancer wears a special mask whose features are grotesquely twisted to one side, supposedly in the likeness of a wealthy local of long ago who

145

suffered from some facial paralysis; copying his appearance is a device to emulate his success in amassing money.

To one side of the forecourt was a tiny shrine hut, and standing on the altar among the standard offerings of fruit and flowers was a curious object that appeared to combine elements of both dances. It was a little horse made from a short, knobbly cucumber with toothpicks stuck in to represent the legs. The front pair had been set on a scrap of dried bark, which had the effect of raising the front of the horse as though it were preparing to set out on a journey. The head—a short section snapped off from the end of another cucumber and impaled on the "shoulders" with another toothpick—seemed to be looking out through the trees and up the road that curved ahead into the mountains. Opening my account for the day with a short prayer, what more natural than to ask if I could clamber up onto its back and take a ride?

Beyond the temple the valley ended abruptly and the road began to climb. In less than a hundred yards the river had narrowed by half and now ran chattering down over smooth brown boulders below a steep, thickly wooded slope. On the opposite verge stood a small orchard of plum trees, each one hung with old cans full of stones to keep the branches growing low. Clusters of new leaves sprouted from the branches on little red stalks, and the young green plums peeped out from among them, no bigger than cherries as yet, but already marked with a soft blush of pink on one side.

At the next corner a deep channel gouged from the top of the embankment to the bottom showed that there had recently been a serious landslip. Nothing had been done to prevent it happening again, but a sturdy barrier of steel girders and heavy wooden boards had been erected to contain the worst of the next fall, whenever it might come, and at least prevent the debris from blocking the road. And after still another long bend I came to the site of a roadside quarry, long disused, with all its sorting and loading apparatus, huge wheels, chutes, and conveyors, rusted, broken, and derelict. Beside a few last piles of rock, now abandoned and overgrown with weeds, the

Ship Horse Picture

river Hamo tumbled cheerfully past and an old wisteria tree bent low over a swirling pool, dripping with bunches of pale, mauvy purple flowers.

The quarry was the last sign of commercial activity, as if the lowlanders ventured this far and no further; beyond, the road narrowed and climbed steeply through deep shadows cast by old cypresses and thickly packed copses of firs. Here and there between their trunks I could make out the shapes of isolated houses, set back from the road and huddled in the half-darkness of somber clearings. Occasionally the road curved and dipped, opening into tiny valley basins where ancient scarecrows stood guard over lilliputian rice paddies lying like droplets of rainwater collected in an upturned leaf; then it plunged on into the shade of the next damp and gloomy patch of forest. On the face of it, there was nothing in these hills to justify the fear voiced by the old innkeeper in Ogi; yet this was undeniably a different world from hers, almost its polar opposite. The towns and villages along the coast gave the impression of being exposed, without secrets, open to their inhabitants and to the elements; gardens lay in full view, clothes fluttered from washing lines, squid and seaweed were hung out on long racks to dry in the sun, windows and doors were left open, and you could look across vistas of fields or far out across the sea. Up here in the mountains, only a short distance away, everything seemed latched or bolted, secretive, clamped down: doors and windows were firmly closed, long heaps of neatly cut firewood lay stacked under low shelters, and plants raised in narrow beds of black soil or gathered from the tangled mountainsides were carried carefully home to be preserved in salt and packed away in jars beneath the farmhouse floor or hung on nails from the rafters of sturdy little barns. Every homestead looked preoccupied with making provision, with laying in stores for the next bout of hard times. Long isolation, it seemed, had bred a kind of siege mentality.

Not that the mountain people were cold or unfriendly; quite the contrary. Those I passed, working in their fields or cutting bamboo along the roadside, greeted me with polite

147

SADO: JAPAN'S ISLAND IN EXILE

interest and no sign of disquiet at my foreign appearance. Once a car pulled up beside me and its driver, a young housewife taking her two young sons to school, leaned across to ask if I wanted a lift. As I thanked her, explaining that I was content to walk, the boys looked up at me with interest from the back seat, clutching their satchels to their chests and smiling shyly from under their yellow school hats. They wanted me on board. It would have been an adventure, something to tell their friends.

After the car had pulled away, I took off my pack and sat in a patch of dappled sunlight by the verge for a rest and a smoke. From up ahead, an old man appeared through the trees, plodding slowly along with the aid of a tall stick. When he saw me, no expression of surprise crossed his face; he stopped, leaned on the stick, and inquired where I was going. Satisfied that my explanation made reasonable sense, he nodded in silence and turned his head away toward the rice paddies on the other side of the road. The skin on his face was deeply lined, his hands were wrinkled, and half his teeth were gone; he wore an old fashioned collarless undervest beneath a frayed jacket, and a battered army cap was perched on top of his narrow head. He was a charcoal maker, he said, just turned seventy, and had been doing the same job for more than fifty years. I asked where he worked, and he waved a hand vaguely at the mountains. "Up there," he said, "in the winter. I used to cut firewood in the summer, but I don't do that any more. I'm not doing anything now." Making charcoal, he explained, was hard, monotonous work: cutting timber from the steep hillsides, roping the logs onto a homemade sledge he had mounted on a pair of cut-down skis, dragging the sledge through the snow to his kiln in a nearby valley, firing the timber, and then waiting till the heat died down and the charcoal was ready to be raked from the kiln and spread out to cool. "There's not much other work to do around here," he said, "and I'm no farmer. Never have been. No land, you see. But I didn't want to move away and live somewhere else. I like it here. So I took up charcoal making. It's best to live where you were born," he added philo-

148

Ship Horse Picture

sophically, "and do your own work in your own time. Not be owned by someone else." I asked what other work options there were locally. "Silkworms," he answered with a shrug. "At least, in the old days. When I was a child, they took over the whole house. There was hardly even any space to sleep—we youngsters used to lie down on the shelves where the trays were, or curl up in any odd corner. In spring we'd cut young shoots from the mulberry trees, and then in the autumn we'd gather whole branches, stripping the leaves off with little blades attached to rings that we wore here," he explained, holding up his two index fingers. "It was a good business when everything went well, but that wasn't often. Too many things to go wrong. You had to give the worms the right amount to eat—not too much and not too little. You had to keep them clean, keep them in the temperature they liked, with the right amount of humidity and everything. After a while, their skin starts to go transparent, and then you have to keep a specially careful eye on them—watching until just the right moment, until they're ready to be moved onto a frame. Then, if we hadn't made any mistakes, they'd settle down happily and start spinning. But like I said, there were just too many things to go wrong . . . and in the end, the business just died. The big firms stopped buying from people like us. They could get silk more easily from foreign countries—China, Korea. They told us it was cheaper, and better quality too. So little by little, everyone around here gave it up. But you have a look as you go along this road. You can still see houses where they used to do it. Some of the bigger ones had a special extra story built on top, just for the silk." He took a last drag on his cigarette and ground the stub into the gravel with a dusty shoe. "Well, I must be getting on," he said. "Take care now!"

At the next village, Osaki, there was a small open square with a new concrete supermarket at one side and a drinks machine by the door where I stopped for another can of iced coffee. Groups of teenage students were gathering in the square and setting off down the hill in twos and threes on their bicycles, heading for school in Hamochi. One of them, bolder

*In the mountains
above Hamochi*

than the rest, came over to me and pointed to a sign beside the shop that read "Bunya Ningyo no Sato." *"Bunya, bunya,"* he urged me. And then, to the accompaniment of guffaws from his pals, he broke into English. "You go now, yes, very good!" An old woman came out of the supermarket carrying a crate of empty beer bottles. "You can't go yet," she said. "It doesn't open until ten o'clock." I decided to skip it, although the museum might well have repaid the wait; Sado's *bunya* has a national reputation and even official designation as An Important Intangible Folk Art. Essentially a rustic version of *bunraku,* Japan's classical puppet theater, it developed a distinctive local character after being brought to Sado from Kyoto in the early seventeenth century. The stories are sung or chanted by a narrator offstage, while puppets, operated by human attendants, perform the action. Originally the stories were expressed in ballads, often with a moral theme, but later the repertoire grew to include specially composed *bunya-bushi,* more complex political tales or war stories. Performances were given at village fairs and temple festivals, but today *bunya* is dying out, shriveled to the status of an occasional, specially staged tourist spectacle.

150

Ship Horse Picture

A little way beyond Osaki, the road climbed a final slope and crossed a level plateau dotted with outcrops of wild flowers—buttercups, yellow chrysanthemums, a few deep blue hyacinths, clumps of ox-eye daisies and orange lilies. It was just nine o'clock when I reached Shimokawamo, the junction with the main route across southern Sado from Akadomari to the central plain. Right on the corner stood a bus stop and hunched over their sticks beside it, like Macbeth's three witches out for a morning excursion, were three old ladies in baggy work trousers and identical olive green cardigans. They called out to me as I went past—What was I doing? Where was I making for? The idea of someone going any distance on foot seemed to astonish them, as though reviving memories from another era. They listened in silence while I explained myself, and when I had finished they threw up their hands in polite amazement and then bowed low in unison, saying *"Gokurosan!"*—"Thank you for taking the trouble!"

It was easy walking to Akadomari, downhill most of the way, and a recent road improvement scheme had added a pavement along one side where I could keep out of the way of the passing traffic—or would have been able to, had any traffic gone by. The banks on each side had been planted with bushes of pink, trumpet-shaped flowers called *utsugi*: the light green, oval-shaped leaves had serrated edges tinged with red, as if dipped in blood, and the flowers grew in tight clusters, twenty or thirty bunched together on a single stem. Passing the last of these bushes, I rounded a corner and found myself beside a deep pond fed by a stream that gushed out between two rocks. Instantly there was a loud plop! followed by several more as a group of frogs, which had been basking in the sun, dove out of sight into the muddy water. Perhaps it was exactly the same experience that inspired the poet Basho to compose his most famous haiku:

> *The old pond*
> *A frog jumps in—*
> *Sound of water.*

151

The coincidence was pleasing and not, I thought, over-presumptuous—although in his book *Zen and Japanese Culture,* D. T. Suzuki warns the "uninitiated" against daring to assume any such mutuality of perception with Japan's greatest poet. "What," he asks, "can most people who are not educated to appreciate a haiku generally see in the enumeration of such familiar objects as an old pond, a jumping frog and the sound resulting therefrom? . . . I am afraid that the uninitiated may not be able to recognize anything poetically enlivening in those seventeen syllables so loosely strung." The answer, I guess, is that you have to be there. For a more encouraging (not to say more cheerful) point of view, you can't do much better than the Zen master Sengai, who lived a century or so later than Basho. One of his paintings shows a frog crouched beneath a banana tree (*basho* in Japanese) with the following haiku brushed above it:

> *If there were a pond here*
> *I'd jump in*
> *So Basho could hear!*

Still chewing over this tasty morsel of Zen humor, I came to Togo-ji, a modest temple set back from the road on a hillside above Akadomari. Tall clumps of yellow and blue irises were growing in a watery garden of rocks and pools, but the temple door was firmly shut and the windows covered with blue-painted shutters, as if the priest and his acolytes had all gone away. Close to the entrance gate was a red *torii* gate and others beyond that with a narrow footpath passing beneath them; the path climbed steeply up to a shrine in the form of a small, glass-fronted hut set on concrete blocks. Inside lay an old drum and two drumsticks, implements for summoning another member of Sado's badger-god family, the *mujina* Zentatsu.

Togo-ji is a Zen temple, and local folklore depicts Zentatsu as an amiable dunce who spent his time making unsuccessful attempts to catch out the abbot with Zen-style questions on the nature of reality. Taking up a position in the kitchen door-

Ship Horse Picture

way one day, he called out, "Hey, Master! What would you say I'm doing—coming in or going out?" Whichever answer the abbot gave, Zentatsu planned to say he meant the other. Instead the abbot picked up a heavy stick and said "Tough question, Zentatsu. Here's another, to help you find the answer yourself. Am I going to hit you over the head with this stick or am I not?" Another time, Zentatsu peeped through the shutters in the early morning and saw the abbot making fire with a flint and steel to light the lanterns for the morning service. "Which one produces the fire?" called out the pesky badger. "The flint or the steel?" "I'll tell you," replied the abbot, "if you can answer this: are you the child of your father or of your mother?" Like other *mujina*, Zentatsu inspires more good-humored tolerance than irritation: even now, the monks of Togo-ji keep a fire burning day and night in the kitchen so that he can come in and warm himself, and every year on September 5 they troop down to his shrine by the gate and conduct a little ceremony in his honor.

* * *

By the time I got down to Akadomari it was close to midday and the sun was burning hot. What I really wanted was a meal, but there was no place to get one: I found three restaurants between one end of town and the other, but with the tourist season not yet under way, they were all firmly closed and shuttered. Even the port was still and quiet except for a group of wiry men in army caps and green rubber boots, who were busy unloading polystyrene boxes of prawns from a fishing boat. Business was evidently good: many of the houses nearby were large and finely built, with deep porches, heavy slatted doors, latticed windows, and newly double-glazed verandahs overlooking well-kept gardens where climbing roses clung to the walls and crimson azaleas flared up from the depths of varnished wooden tubs. One verandah had a long bamboo pole slung between two supports: at one end was the family washing while at the other were three huge fish, of different varieties, gutted and hung up by strings through their gills to dry in the sun.

153

SADO: JAPAN'S ISLAND IN EXILE

Next door, the neighbors were building a garage: ready-mixed concrete was being unloaded from a mixer truck under the supervision of a thin-faced man who slouched against the door-post with a cigarette glued to his bottom lip, while a woman who was sixty if she was a day labored away bent double, spreading out the heavy gray sludge with a shovel.

Eventually I found a small food store that sold me two rice balls and a large can of beer, which I consumed while looking in at the window of a nearby carpenter's shop. The owner was preparing planks of cedar with a long wooden plane, leaning into his strokes and singing along with the radio at the top of his voice. Above his head, several bunches of onions dangled from nails driven into the beams of the ceiling. When I called out and asked him for some water to refill my empty bottle, he stopped planing and looked at me suspiciously, then pointed to a long coil of green hose attached to a tap by the door. He watched while I filled the bottle, and then, without asking my destination, pointed down the road that led out of town. "That way," he said urgently, "that's the way for you!"

A signpost announced that the distance to Oda, the next place of any size, was exactly eight kilometers, or about five miles. For no particular reason, this suddenly struck me as an immensely long way. The sun was still blazing down, I was tired from walking through the mountains, my feet hurt, and I could see the road stretching ahead along a coast as empty and desolate as on the day of creation; on one side an unscalable wall of steep cliff and on the other an empty expanse of glittering blue sea. The idea began to come over me that I was entirely alone here, that there was no one around, nor ever had been, or that at least all the local inhabitants had gone away in a body, perhaps to avoid some impending calamity of which only I was ignorant. No traffic passed by in either direction, no children played in the cottage gardens, no graybeards sat out in the sunshine, no one was working in the fields—there were no fields—and no birds flew past in the sky, not a seagull, not a kite, not even a crow. Trudging along with my head down, I passed into a kind of stupor tinged with melancholy. For the first time since

154

Ship Horse Picture

starting this journey I felt a sense of the sadness of Sado, island of exile, dumping ground for Japan's Unwanted, and of the peculiar desolation in which they dug in, waited, and hoped— many to molder and die, only a few to survive and return home. Scratching out a daily existence was a full-time occupation, an achievement in itself, made harder and lonelier by the perception of spiritual doom, of remorse, guilt, and shame, of agonized longings, bitter memories, blighted destinies. Whatever their situation, many exiles must have at least started out with hope and resolution, fired perhaps by the bitterness of perceived injustice, thirsty for revenge, determined to survive and one day recover their place in the world . . . but as months and years went by and no hint of pardon came, the realization would have grown that they were truly abandoned, that exile meant more than separation from society—it meant oblivion. In time, as memories dimmed, ties with the past began to fray and snap; the tough business of daily survival would absorb all their attention, bitterness would fade, vengefulness dissolve, hopes decay. To an educated, sophisticated individual, the mental damage would be severe and permanent; descending at a stroke from the heights of privilege to a life no better than a goat's, deprived of familiar culture, quarantined from all intercourse, and condemned into the bargain to cold, hunger, and fear, the mind would shut down or go mad. Skills and abilities withered from disuse, forms of behavior lost their relevance, blocks of knowledge fell away from the brain like pillars of ice crumbling from the face of a glacier into the sea.

There was no sound in the still air but my own labored breathing and the sharp, regular clunk! of my stick on the tarmac. Rain-blackened wooden shacks sagging with age, nets spread out to dry on the seawall, battered dinghies drawn up on the shingle, all passed me by as though in a film, as though I was watching all this happen to someone else. And it was while I was in this soporific state, not miserable exactly but weary and dulled, that my eye was suddenly caught by a movement on the road and I stopped in my tracks as if frozen.

It was a snake, not three feet in front of me, with half its

155

body in the grassy verge and the rest stretched out across the asphalt to investigate what looked like a dead vole. Dark, fat, and shiny, it had distinctive markings along its back, but I couldn't remember what they signified: was it the poisonous *mamushi* or some other, harmless species? I had come across some fairly big snakes before in Japan, though not on Sado, but this was a whopper—six or eight feet long, perhaps more—how much was hidden in the grass?—and as thick as a good-size drainpipe. In a flash, my torpor evaporated. I was as wide awake and tightly wound as a spy crawling at night through an enemy camp. For a few interminable seconds we stared at each other without moving; then I gingerly took a couple of paces back, gripping Snake Frightener with both hands and wondering whether I would do better to try and get in a good clout on its head or simply fling away the stick and run for my life.

Neither expedient proved necessary: as I moved back, the snake unfroze and began to turn away. Raising the front half of its body slightly from the ground, it swung round 180 degrees toward the verge, undulating and slithering as its glossy scales struggled for purchase on the paper-flat tarmac of the road. In what must have been only a few short seconds, it had slid away and disappeared into the coarse grass with a whispery rustle, as smoothly as toothpaste squeezed from a giant's tube.

For a long moment after it had gone, I stood there holding Snake Frightener in a tight grip. Several times over the last few days I had teased myself for the slightly ludicrous, even melodramatic, conceit of carrying along this pilgrim's staff, and more than once had been made to feel sheepish by the good-humored banter of others. Not any more. No sir, not for another second. Without any doubt it was the sound of the stick that had told the snake I was coming and caused it to make that first slight movement that had caught my eye. But for that I would certainly have taken one more step and trodden right on its sleek, fat body before realizing it was there.

A good sharp fright changes everything, and I walked on in a completely renewed and cheerful frame of mind. Now it seemed that there *were* birds and flowers around after all, and

Ship Horse Picture

people too: as I came abreast of a substantial modern house fronted with large picture windows, a battered blue pickup pulled off the road into the driveway and a middle-aged couple got out and bade me a cheerful greeting. "My, you look hot and tired!" exclaimed the woman. "Here, come inside with us and take a rest. We've got some *warabi*—look, we've just been up to pick it in the mountains!" And she held out a piece of newspaper on which lay a small pile of little green plants that looked like young shoots of bracken.

The house was an inn, and although they hadn't yet opened for the season, the man said they would gladly put me up if I wanted to stay for a few days. While the wife scuttled about preparing the *warabi* and bringing ice-cold cans of beer from the fridge, the husband dug an old school atlas out of a cupboard and fumbled for his glasses. "America," he muttered as he thumbed slowly through the pages, "America . . . now where has it gone? Ah! Here it is. America. And here," he added triumphantly, pointing with his finger, "is Ohio. Ohio is a state. There's a university there. That's where our son is, right now. He's studying English. When he comes back, he's going to be a high school teacher."

I thought they might be disappointed to find that I wasn't American and had never even been to Ohio, but it didn't really register. As a foreigner, they expected me to know all about it anyway. I struggled to remember something—anything would do. There was a big river in Ohio, I knew that. And steel mills. Pittsburgh—was that right? Or was that Pennsylvania? And that other place—what was it called? Ah yes, Cleveland! They were pleased when I mentioned Cleveland. And presidents. More American presidents had come from Ohio than from any other state. That must signify something. But what? And anyway, which ones were they? I couldn't recall a single one. But it didn't matter. I was a foreigner—an honorary American. By showing hospitality to me, they could pay something back to all the nameless residents of Ohio who were even then showering their son with kindness and generosity.

While we ate the *warabi* and drank the beer, the wife

157

SADO: JAPAN'S ISLAND IN EXILE

Street in Oda

announced that they had a dog that could sing. I had already noticed a sandy colored mutt out in the yard—I was keeping half an eye on it because it had come over to the verandah a couple of times to have a good sniff of my boots, and I wanted to make sure it didn't piss on them as well. "You watch," she said. "I'll just tell it to sing, and then it will. Go on, then!" she called. "Sing!" And sure enough, the dog stood back, threw his muzzle up vertically toward the sky, opened his jaws, and let out a ghastly, high-pitched, crooning wail. "Do it again!" commanded his mistress, as the sound died away. So the dog did it again.

"That's enough now," interrupted the husband. "It's time for that TV program. Let's switch it on." So we all poured out more beer and swiveled round to face the TV. At first, I couldn't understand what was going on—the program seemed to be some kind of sales pitch, delivered by a matronly lady in a white pharmacist's uniform. For the first few minutes, her ample face filled the screen, but then the camera panned back to show her standing by a table and introducing the products. They were all items

158

Ship Horse Picture

of equipment to cope with incontinence in the elderly: bottles and tubes, balloon-like undergarments, folded pieces of soft plastic, absorbent pads, and mysteriously shaped containers.

The husband watched with rapt attention, but his wife soon got bored. "Have you got a map?" she asked me. "You can't walk about on Sado without a map, you know." I assured her that I had a map, but she didn't take any notice. "Here, you can have this one," she said, reaching for a brochure that lay on top of a pile of magazines. "It's the one we give to all the guests who stay here. Otherwise they wouldn't know where to go, would they?" She opened the brochure out on the table. It showed a schematic outline of Sado with smiling little cartoon fish marking the best fishing places, smiling little swimmers indicating the best bathing places, and brightly colored little boats showing where you could catch a tourist launch and go out sightseeing along the coast. As a map for driving it was useless and for walking, completely useless. I thanked her profusely and stowed it carefully away in a pocket of my pack.

The sun was still blazing out of the mid-afternoon sky when I left the inn and walked on down into the village of Oda. I had intended to find a room there for the night, but everything was closed and silent. From the far end of the single street a trail led off into the mountains, roughly concreted and wide enough for the passage of a car; but ahead along the coast, perhaps a mile further on, I could see a headland jutting out into the sea, with a white lighthouse and a beach that looked good for camping. Along the way, beside a group of tiny, solemn Jizo statues that had been decapitated and then inexpertly repaired, lay the body of a creature run over by a passing car. Most of the flesh had already been picked from the bones, but from the scraps of fur left on the face and tail I saw that it was a *tanuki;* it had paws like a dog, with curved claws, and its lips were drawn back as though smiling, displaying a mouthful of broken teeth.

A road sign by the headland was inscribed with the name Matsugasaki ("Pine Headland"). There was a temple with a massive old tree in the courtyard, and a shop that sold packets

159

SADO: JAPAN'S ISLAND IN EXILE

of dried food, vegetables, ice cream, chewing gum, and, to my surprise, a few dusty bottles of cheap French wine. Between the shop and the temple, a footpath led out to the shingle beach. Driftwood lay scattered about in piles thrown up by the sea, so making a fire would be no problem: there were even a couple of brick-built barbecues set up on a grassy knoll that served as an official picnic area. It was a perfect place to camp.

Drawing the cork on my bottle of wine, I looked out at the sea and listened to the waves as they lapped at the gray stones. Now I remembered where I had heard of Matsugasaki before: it was the place where Sado's most famous exile had landed at the start of his sentence—Nichiren, the *enfant terrible* of Buddhist history. Back near Sawada I had visited a temple where he was supposed to have stayed; but that was a later chapter in his story. The person who stumbled ashore at Matsugasaki was very different—condemned, cold, exhausted, and filled with despair.

Nichiren's journey into history began on February 16, 1222, when he was born in a tiny fishing hamlet called Komina-to, on the Pacific coast of the Chiba peninsula, east of Tokyo. Even today's overlay of asphalt roads, vending machines, and convenience stores does little to hide the village's simple character. On one side, a long beach scattered with seaweed, driftwood, and broken crab shells, where as a child Nichiren helped his father and the other local fishermen to haul their boats out of the surf, repair their nets, and hang up the lamps for another night at sea. On the other, a daunting landscape of steep, knobbly mountains, completely covered with trees and scrub and so close together as to leave only the narrowest patches of valley floor for cultivation.

The boy showed early signs of an intelligent, questioning character, and in 1233, when he was eleven, his father sent him to start a religious training at Seicho-ji, a temple in the hills behind his village. Here he learned to read and write and studied the doctrines of Tendai Buddhism. He was evidently a bright student, taking his vows of ordination only four years later and being given the name "Rencho," or "Lotus Eternal."

160

Ship Horse Picture

But life in the rustic temple soon began to chafe, and in his mid-teens he decided to go out into the world and "study all the branches of Buddhism known in Japan."

At sixteen, he set off on a pilgrimage that lasted for ten years and took him to many important Buddhist centers, including the great Tendai complex of red-painted wooden temples on Mt. Hiei, above Kyoto. What he saw on his travels convinced him that something in Japan was badly wrong. All the established sects of Buddhism danced on strings held in the hands of the aristocracy. Of the young acolytes in each temple, it was always the well born who were marked out for favor and promotion. Buddhist practice, too, seemed over-complex, finicky, and elitist. Resentful and dissatisfied, he sought a more straightforward route to salvation, one which everyone, even the poorly educated, could undertake. Out of this quest emerged one overriding conviction—that the supreme truth was to be found in the words of the *Lotus Sutra*. The sutra's title is the phrase *myoho renge kyo*, which means something like "the scripture of the Lotus of Perfect Truth," and the essential core of everyday religious practice, according to Nichiren, was repetition of this formula prefixed by the Sanskrit word *namu*, which signifies devotion. Chanting it over and over again would concretize the worshipper's allegiance to the truths which the sutra revealed. This was a landmark in his thinking, and he commemorated it by changing his own name from Rencho to Nichiren, which means "Sun Lotus."

To test his ideas, he returned to his birthplace and paid a visit to his old master and fellow monks at Seicho-ji. Here he expounded the new doctrine, declaring it to be not merely an improvement on all other forms of Buddhism, but the only antidote to their heresies. The effect was the opposite of what he intended: his hearers were offended and took him for a simpleton. And when word of the incident reached Tojo Kagenobu, the local lord, he flew into a temper. Orders were given for the blasphemer to be killed at once. But the death squad arrived too late: Nichiren's friends took pity on him and managed to arrange an ignominious escape through the forest.

161

SADO: JAPAN'S ISLAND IN EXILE

Disappointed but not disheartened, he embarked on missionary journeys through other nearby provinces before finally settling in a town just south of Edo called Kamakura, which was then the seat of government. Here he embarked on his dangerous lifelong habit of writing open letters to the ruling authorities, harshly criticizing their policies and recommending—later demanding—that they adopt his own suggestions instead. His first petition, presented in July 1260, was entitled "The Establishment of Righteousness and the Security of the Country,", which shows that he was not a man to go for small themes. But his criticisms displeased the authorities, and shortly afterward, probably at their instigation, Nichiren's hermitage was attacked by a mob and burnt down.

Buddhism was already well established in Japan, having been imported by priests and scholars who had studied in China or Korea and then returned to set up schools and temples of their own. By and large they adopted a good-neighbor policy toward each other, so that different sects with their own individual variations flourished at the same time. Sensibly regarding none of these versions as definitive, the secular and ecclesiastical authorities allowed all of them to take root and flower side by side. But as general learning spread and grew, so did the differences between the sects—degrees of popularity, numbers of adherents, influence at court, material wealth. Many were blatantly corrupt, and some of the most powerful temples maintained armies of priest-warriors called *sohei*, with which they conducted raids and even prolonged wars against their rivals. The young Nichiren thought them immoral, lazy, spiritually weak, parasites on the people. And by the time he took up residence in Kamakura, it seemed to him that the same situation had arisen that always arises when religious big shots eat too much, drink too much, sleep too much, and have too much money and not enough useful work to do. Other people, he found, felt the same way. They shared his belief that the Age of Mappo had come, the prophesied time when virtue would decline and moral degeneration would spread throughout society.

162

Ship Horse Picture

And was it a coincidence that Japan was suffering such an unprecedented number of natural disasters? Certainly the thirteenth century had more than its share: devastating typhoons, catastrophic earthquakes, fires that gutted whole cities, and, more than once, famines which so weakened the people that human and animal corpses lay unburied beside the roads. To Nichiren, these events had an ominous significance: they were directly caused by the nation's spiritual decay. As usual, there would be nothing for the poor to do except die, or grow poorer. The rich and well-connected could sit it out in their castles and their palaces, attending to the fashionable preoccupations of the day. Conventional Buddhism could skulk in its gilded temples, devising ever more abstract concepts and abstruse rituals. But nothing would change for the better until control of the country was wrested from the military usurpers in Kamakura and a new wave of religious purity cleansed the land.

In fact, things might easily get worse. For instance, what if Kublai Khan, lord of the mighty Mongol empire, took it into his head to add Japan to his possessions? Nichiren's first warning on this subject, issued in 1260, was ignored. But when in 1268 it became known that Kublai Khan actually had such a plan, and had dispatched envoys precisely for the purpose of demanding official submission from Japan and the payment of tribute, the result was something like panic. Nichiren was astute enough to realize what thanks he could expect. "We are likely to face prosecution," he wrote in a circular letter to his small band of followers, "with either exile or death as the outcome. You must not be surprised."

Meanwhile his denunciations of other Buddhist forms of worship increased in scorn and bile. The teachings of the Pure Land sect he dismissed as a direct route to hell. Zen was the teaching of demons. Shingon was obsessed with pageantry. Ritsu was directly to blame for natural calamities. This aggressive mode of argument was, as he admitted, a deliberate tactic. "Strong remonstrances have been made on purpose," the same letter adds, "in order to awaken the people."

Absenting himself from Kamakura for a year after his hut

163

SADO: JAPAN'S ISLAND IN EXILE

was burnt down, Nichiren returned in 1261 and was promptly arrested and banished to the Izu peninsula, three or four days' journey to the south. There he stayed until the beginning of 1263, when for reasons that are not known, the banishment order was lifted. In April he returned to a warm welcome from his followers in Kamakura, but ignored their pleas to change his tone and act more moderately.

So why did they stick by him? Obviously because his teaching carried conviction. To know the *Lotus Sutra*, he declared, was to understand the true character of the Buddha. This had not been an ordinary man, as others claimed, who had been born in central India and just went around teaching the simple elements of a simple faith. Nor was he a superman with miraculous powers, offering enlightenment as a reward for devotion. Nichiren's Buddha was beyond either of these. He was the Great Self of the Universe, a sort of immanent god; through him, everything and everyone, however humble or insignificant, shared the same divine nature. "Behold!" Nichiren could have said in another time and place, "the kingdom of God is within you!"

Another reason for his success must have been the sheer force of his personality. No convention was too sacred for criticism. One that particularly irked him was the idea that women were intrinsically inferior to men, that their acts of worship should be bound by special restrictions. In 1263, he received a letter from a female follower—and the fact that it was written at all says a lot about his character—asking about the rules that she should observe during her monthly period. At the time, menstruating women were regarded as polluted and were forbidden to approach sacred places. Nichiren wrote back that no special precautions were necessary. She should worship and recite the scriptures as usual. If she had any scruples about uncleanliness, he added, she need not actually hold the scriptures in her hand: it would suffice to pronounce the words. This combination of delicacy toward the individual and indifference to established norms was, to say the least, unusual.

In the autumn of 1264, Nichiren heard that his mother

164

Ship Horse Picture

was ill, so he set out to pay her a last visit. When he arrived, he found her close to death, but his prayers had some effect—or so he believed—because she gradually recovered and lived on for another four years. Full of faith in his own powers, Nichiren again paid a visit to his old teacher at Seicho-ji, hoping this time to convert him. Again, the visit was a failure. Moved to tears, the old man thanked Nichiren for his efforts but declined to change course so late in life. This disappointment was quickly followed by near-disaster: no sooner had Nichiren and his followers left the temple than they were waylaid by servants of the same local lord who had tried to kill him before. This time there was a fight, involving (according to Nichiren) "hundreds of attackers whose arrows fell from the sky like rain and whose swords clashed like lightning. One of my followers was killed, two were badly injured, and I myself was struck on the forehead and also on the left hand. It seemed there would be no escape, yet somehow I was saved. How, I cannot explain."

165

DAY 7

BALL OF FIRE

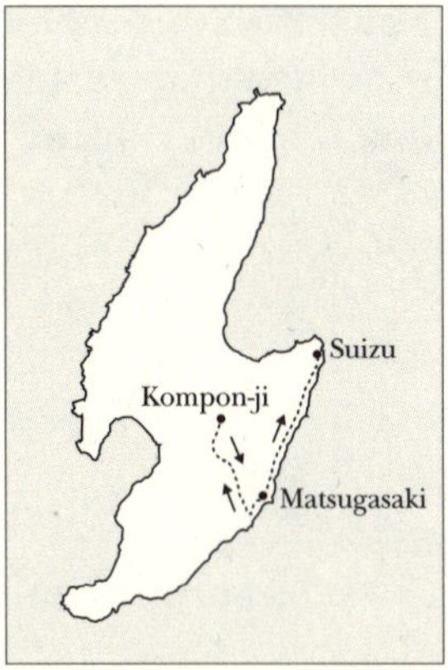

Details of his life for the next four years are sketchy, but in 1268 Nichiren was certainly back in Kamakura because that was the year in which Kublai Khan sent envoys to demand Japan's submission. "Recall the warning I gave eight years ago!" wrote Nichiren in another of his open letters. "Is it not now coming true? Is there anyone but I who can repel this danger to our country? Only one who knows the real cause of a situation can influence its outcome." This appeal, like its predecessors, went unanswered, so Nichiren stepped up a couple of gears and dispatched a total of eleven letters simultaneously to government officials and to the abbots of leading monasteries. What happened next is not recorded: probably Kamakura became too hot to hold him, as he dropped out of sight again.

By 1270 he was back, as truculent as ever. This time his principal target was Ryokuan, the popular abbot of Gokuraku Temple and an associate of the ruling Hojo family. That summer there was a severe drought, and Ryokuan let it be known

166

Ball of Fire

that he was performing special prayers and rituals to bring rain. When these efforts failed, Nichiren derided Ryokuan as a charlatan, angering the abbot's supporters at court. At the same time he fell out with a prominent courtier called Hei no Saemon, a relative of the Hojo and a follower of Amidha, the Buddha of the Pure Land sect. Nichiren insulted this man in a succession of aggressive letters, eventually provoking him to seek judicial satisfaction. A summons was issued, ordering Nichiren to appear in court on October 15 and justify his slanderous attacks.

Characteristically, the fisherman's son who once described himself as "the most intractable man in Japan" responded by firing off yet another broadside. This time, it was one too many. On the morning of October 17, a troop of soldiers came to arrest him. At their head strode Hei no Saemon, "wearing the headgear of a court noble, glaring angrily and giving orders in a fierce tone of voice."

The trial was held immediately: the charge was treason and the sentence was banishment to Sado. A curious juridical twist, not uncommon at the time, left the manner of the prisoner's journey into exile and his fate in the meantime in the hands of the individual technically responsible for bringing the charge—in this case, Hei no Saemon. There wasn't much doubt as to what Nichiren could expect.

That evening, Nichiren was mounted on a horse and paraded round Kamakura so that his downfall should become known. After midnight, the party moved off along the coast road to what is now Koshigoe, a village close to Enoshima, where there was a public execution ground known as Tatsunokuchi ("Mouth of the Dragon"). There, the scene was set for a theatrical revenge. Armed soldiers stood guard, the executioner held his sword at the ready, and Hei no Saemon watched impassively from the official witness's chair. Realizing that the end had come, Nichiren knelt down on the tatami mat spread out for him, put his hands together and spoke the words of his final prayer.

Then, quite suddenly (according to Nichiren's own account), "a ball of fire as bright as the moon flew across the

167

SADO: JAPAN'S ISLAND IN EXILE

sky over the island of Enoshima," lighting up the scene so that everyone's face was clearly visible. The dazzled executioner staggered, dropped his sword, and fell to the ground. The soldiers were terrified, running this way and that in panic or prostrating themselves while still in the saddle. Order degenerated into chaos, and the execution was abandoned.

Fearing that divine intervention had been the cause, the authorities were in some confusion about what to do next. But the decision was not long in coming. The original sentence of the court was reaffirmed. Nichiren was detained near Kamakura, while travel preparations were made. One month later he set out for Sado.

It was an arduous eleven-day walk to the Japan Sea coast and the little beachside port of Teradomari ("Temple-Stay"), from which ferries to Sado still sail today. Winter was well under way and the weather was bad: the party had to wait for a further week in Teradomari before they could attempt the crossing. While they were at sea, another storm blew up, this time from the south; blown off course, they missed Akadomari, Teradomari's corresponding port on Sado, and made landfall a few miles to the north, on the stony beach at Matsugasaki.

* * *

Another cool, sunny dawn greeted me as I crawled out of my sleeping bag at first light and sat on the grassy knoll with a cup of tea. Behind me among the trees stood the temple I had seen the night before—the same temple, or rather the same temple site, where Nichiren and his military escort supposedly spent their first night on Sado, with the prisoner himself sleeping out in the open at the foot of a zelkova tree. When I walked round to take a look, I found a signboard on which were painted the words

NICHIRENSHU
THEHONGYOJI
TEMPLL

168

Ball of Fire

Sure enough there was a huge old zelkova in the court-yard, but as seven hundred years had elapsed since Nichiren's visit, there didn't seem much likelihood of its being the same one. But when I examined it I wasn't so sure. The trunk was truly massive, eight or ten feet in diameter at the base and divided into a giant fork about twelve feet off the ground. The bark was made up of thick, chunky plates divided by deep cracks, like the roughly chapped hide of a prehistoric monster.

Whether it was the original tree or not, this was evidently Nichiren's place of arrival. From here he had a further journey to make across the mountains to his final destination on the Kuninaka plain. If the party had arrived at the port they intend-ed, their route would have taken them over the same road I had followed down into Akadomari the day before. As it was, they were too far north to make the detour worthwhile, so instead they took the mountain trail out of Oda village, which bore the same name then as it does today—Matsugasaki Kaido, or "Pine Headland Road." That meant starting off with a walk along what must have been little more than a footpath at the base of the cliff, freezing cold in the December gale, probably in a swirl of snow, and traveling for an unknown distance to an unknown place of detention.

My own plan had been to continue north along the coast, but since the weather was fine and I was in no particular hurry, I decided to make a detour of my own and retrace the exile's route. Back in Oda I turned off the main road and took the concrete-paved trail along the bank of a stream and up toward the mountains. On one side stood the village school, its play-ground bordered with cherry trees, and on the other a small sawmill where a clean, fresh smell wafted out from a newly cut stack of heavy pine boards. A few frogs were having an early-morning rumble by the edges of the paddies and from a tele-graph wire above my head came the guttural bark of a crow. Two old women in white bonnets and short rubber boots were already at work in a field, tipping tiny heaps of powdered fertil-izer out of a bucket and raking them over the dark soil.

Beyond the last houses, the Matsugasaki Kaido described

169

a long curve to the left, skirting a group of paddies, and then disappeared into the forest. The pass ahead was neither far nor high, but the climb was steep: here and there among the trees I could see glimpses of the road, which snaked its way up in long loops to right and left. By the look of it, several miles of uphill walking lay ahead, so I stopped and dug out the map to see if there might be any alternative. Sure enough, two other tracks were marked, both with steeper gradients but both cutting off a lot of distance, so I took the first one I came to, turning off the road beside a concrete bridge. This new route began as a paved road but reverted to an unmade track within a couple of hundred yards and narrowed sharply as it climbed up into a deeply shaded gully beside a tumbling stream. Soon it was no more than a footpath; here and there it crossed and recrossed the stream on fantastic old log bridges, rotten to the heart and with a profusion of flowers and grasses growing out of their sides like mops of tangled hair.

After a while the path turned away from the stream, climbed through some trees, and crossed over a grassy shoulder of the mountain to a dilapidated farm where a hunchbacked old woman was busily weeding a small vegetable patch. She raised her head and nodded politely, but without curiosity, as I passed. Farming up here on this exposed, steeply sloping escarpment looked like a strictly subsistence affair; there were a few small paddies on carefully cut terraces, a fenced-in area of stone-bordered beds for vegetables, a few peach trees, and a little black hut fronted by a wire chicken run. Two white ducks with brilliant orange beaks waddled quickly ahead of me along the path and flapped to one side as I went by.

The path continued to climb, mostly enclosed by trees—pine, chestnut, ash, and an occasional wild cherry—and with so many twists and turns, to say nothing of intersections with other trails, that I kept losing my sense of direction and had to keep checking the map. The accuracy of detail in Japanese maps tends to be patchy at best, but this one had it about right: the path turned obediently east and west where bends were marked and changes in gradient matched the contour lines. Certainly I

Ball of Fire

could never have found my way without it: many of the inter-
secting trails were omitted for the simple reason that they had
never been surveyed. It's easy to think that satellites have solved
the problem of surveying on the ground, and it's true that the
general picture they give has taken some of the work out of
modern mapmaking. But every landscape has some features
that don't show up on satellite photos—a path through woods
is an obvious example—and others that can be seen but not
identified (is it a house? a hotel? a post office?). To get the job
right you need corroborative surveying on the ground, and
although the tangled mountains of Sado are less rugged than
ranges elsewhere in Japan, it would still take a hundred surveyors a hundred years to map them properly. Which makes it a
job that's never going to get done.

A long, straight stretch followed by a sharp dogleg, faith-
fully marked, turned up on cue, and I came out of the woods
onto another steep escarpment. At its foot, among flowering
azalea and dangling bunches of purple wisteria, stood another
decrepit-looking farmhouse. Oddly angled timbers provided a
frame for cracked and flaking wattle-and-daub walls, tall bunches of grass sprouted from the mangy thatched roof, and a thin
plume of smoke curled up into the sky from a crooked chimney. Surrounded by nothing but forest, it looked like the original witch's cottage; for a few moments I stood and stared, as
though waiting for a crone in a pointed black hat to hobble out
and put a spell on me. But then I spotted a single telegraph
wire leading from its terminal under the eaves up into the trees
ahead; and following its course I scrambled up the last couple
of hundred yards of my shortcut and came back out onto the
Matsugasaki Kaido by a small wrecking yard with the rusty
corpses of a dozen cars piled together beside a tin shed. There
was even an automatic drinks machine by the road with a line
of winking red lights along the front panel, inviting me to
insert a 100-yen coin and sample the delights of Lotte orange
juice; but when I complied, nothing happened.

The top of the pass was now only a mile or two ahead and
the road wound gently up toward it through a forest of pines

171

whose tawny orange trunks were streaked with shadows cast by their own branches. There was little traffic, but the road had been widened here and there so that cars could pass—mostly by blasting chunks out of the mountainside on the sharpest corners. The summit itself was entirely enclosed by trees, so that there was no view in any direction, but I stopped to pass the time of day with an old man who had toiled up from the other side in the company of a ragged, gray-brown mongrel with a long, brushlike tail. The man lived on the central plain, in the town of Hatano, but had been making this journey on foot for years, ever since he had started courting his wife, who was born on the coast in Oda. The idea of a foreigner walking around Sado for pleasure struck him as highly amusing. "What are you carrying that stick for?" he wanted to know. I told him it was to protect myself from fierce dogs, and he cackled so loudly that his shoulders shook. "No need for that," he gasped between spasms. "You won't be bothered by dogs here. Not this one, anyway. He's never bitten anyone in his life." Ha ha! Of course not. I was only kidding. Except that—what was it I read in that old book about travel in Japan? "The Japanese dog," wrote the author, F. W. Brinkley, "is a valueless brute. A few months of life suffice to convert him into an ill-shapen, unsightly and useless cur." Of course Brinkley was writing in the wild old days of the nineteenth century, so he wasn't around when pets in Japan ceased being animals and evolved into fashion accessories. He was too early for the era of the pampered poodle, the carefully groomed beagle pup, the mollycoddled chihuahua, and the plastic pooper scooper. But on Sado, that era had not yet begun. From what I had seen, most of the island dogs were the Brinkley type. I eyed the old man's mutt and it glowered back at me, panting, with a long pink tongue dangling from one side of its slavering jaws.

Seven hundred years ago, when Nichiren came this way in the freezing cold of early winter, dogs were probably the least of his worries. After toiling up to the top of the pass, he came down alongside the Ogura River and stopped to rest at a place called Omedo. I did the same, slumping on the ground by a

Ball of Fire

Roadside Jizo

huge slab of granite set up to mark his passage. Across the road, the river had been dammed to make a small reservoir for the settlements in the valley below; yellow irises were growing in patches around its banks and an old wisteria dangled its flowers over the surface of the muddy water. There were houses around now, one with the windows already flung wide and a leathery-skinned old man lying on the floor with his head on a small pillow, dozing in the warm, early morning sun.

Two hours down from the top of the pass, I came to Chokoku-ji, a grand old temple approached up a long flight of wide stone steps flanked by two massive cedars at the entrance. The grounds were crowded with stone lanterns, Jizo statues, and engraved tombstones, all surveyed from the top of a plinth by an image of Fudo Myoo, the "Immovable Wisdom King" and patron of the *yamabushi.* The statue portrayed a ferocious character scowling angrily, with one fang pointing down and another up, a braid hanging down one side of the head, holding a sword, and surrounded by leaping flames. Fudo is a familiar sight in remote parts of Japan; travelers come across his images along rocky shores, beside waterfalls, in deep gorges, and little-visited mountain valleys. He is an aspect of Avalokitesvara, the Bodhisattva of Compassion, and his fierce aspect, somewhat paradoxically, denotes his opposition to violence and his determination to quell it wherever it occurs.

At the top of the steps, beside the main temple, was a structure like a miniature sports stadium, and inside, completely filling several long shelves, stood hundreds of stone Jizo.

173

They looked exactly like a crowd at a soccer match, the more so because all their faces were different: some had round heads like Halloween pumpkins, some looked wasted and thin, some were smiling cheerfully, some stared coldly ahead with severe or gloomy expressions, and a few were praying with heads angled slightly forward and their little hands clasped around strings of stone beads. Having come to the temple as a visitor, I felt more as if the roles had been reversed, as if they were spectators awaiting some sort of performance from me.

Whether Nichiren stopped off at Chokoku-ji is not recorded; if so, it must only have been a brief visit because his guards had orders to deliver him without delay to a village called Tsukahara. Here, it was hoped, he would soon die—and the place of detention at Tsukahara, namely the local cemetery, was just the spot to set the mood. Most of the dead were interred in the usual way, but the bodies of paupers and executed criminals, which no one had either the money or the inclination to bury, were simply dumped on open ground and left to rot where they lay. There was a small, semiderelict hut on the site and this was where Nichiren and his one permitted companion were installed.

That first winter, with little to eat and only straw and rags to ward off the cold, their situation was desperate. A letter scribbled two months after his arrival describes the exile's first impressions. "An icy wind blows here all the time," he wrote, "and although there are some days when the snow does not fall, we never catch so much as a glimpse of the sun. The mountains are infested with robbers; the seas are alive with pirates. The local people are as savage as wild animals. They know nothing of ethical standards, not even the most basic. How could they tell the difference between heresy and truth, between a good teacher and a bad one?"

Another note, written at about the same time, struck an even more hopeless tone. "A man called Nichiren was taken to Tatsunokuchi at midnight on the twelfth day of the ninth month last year. There he was beheaded, but his soul remained and afterward came here to the island of Sado. It wrote these

Ball of Fire

words, surrounded by snow, in the second month of the following year, and leaves them to posterity."

It is very likely that Nichiren would not have survived that first winter had he not been saved by a characteristic incident in which he won over an enemy who wanted to kill him. An ardent Pure Lander, this man decided to get rid of Nichiren for good and took to hanging around the hut armed with a sword, looking for a suitable opportunity. But after a while he began to feel ashamed of lurking in the bushes, waiting for a chance to kill an unarmed man; and when he overheard Nichiren reciting the scriptures, he decided to try reason instead of violence. Face to face, he would argue things out and cure the dissident of his errors. Of course, the outcome was the opposite: Nichiren soon converted the man, whose name was Abutsubo, and also his wife, Sennichini. The couple then took on the dangerous responsibility of supplying Nichiren with food. In a letter written to Sennichini some years later, Nichiren remembered their courage and their kindness. "The authorities and the Amidhists kept watch to stop anyone visiting my hut," he wrote, "but you loaded food onto Abutsubo's back and sent him to me time and again during the night. I felt as if my own dear mother had been reborn there on Sado."

Other people on Sado also had plans for disposing of the newly arrived heretic. Some of the local priests favored the direct method: they wanted to take advantage of his unprotected status and put him to death. So they approached the local lord, Homma Rokurozaemon, and asked him to do the job for them. But he refused to allow it, telling the priests he had received an official government directive that specifically stated Nichiren should not be harmed. Instead of an execution, he proposed a debate. That way, Nichiren's poisonous doctrines could be exposed to the public ridicule they deserved.

After some consideration, the priests accepted this suggestion and the debate was arranged. A large crowd attended—ecclesiastics of all ranks from the island's temples and monasteries, Homma Rokurozaemon, several local notables, and a good-sized lay audience as well. Naturally, the situation

175

SADO: JAPAN'S ISLAND IN EXILE

was meat and drink to an experienced debater like Nichiren. "One by one, my adversaries came forward and expounded their doctrines," he reported later, "while I patiently answered them in turn, establishing precisely what their propositions were and then cross-examining them. I only needed to ask one or two questions at the most to shut them up completely. They were quite pathetic, far inferior even to the priests in Kamakura—I defeated them as easily as a sword cutting through a melon. In their ignorance, they muddled not only quotations but also sources of doctrine, unable to distinguish between sutras, treatises, and commentaries. As I demonstrated their errors, some exclaimed in amazement while others turned pale and could not answer. Some even renounced their beliefs on the spot, taking off their robes and beads and throwing them on the ground."

The tide of Nichiren's affairs had started to turn, and when spring came round, a new optimism bloomed with it. The official restrictions on his life were eased; he was allowed to move from Tsukahara to a village called Ichinosawa, where he became the houseguest of a prosperous local farmer. Every morning he walked down the hill to the little temple of Jisso-ji to greet the rising sun, and although he complained that "there is very little writing paper here on Sado," he managed to acquire enough to begin composing his well-known mandalas, in which the names of Buddhas, boddhisatvas, and other aspects of the godhead are inscribed in a circular form around the familiar title phrase of the *Lotus Sutra.*

From time to time he engaged in fresh debates with the local monks, which usually led to him gaining new converts. After 1272, he was allowed to begin receiving visits from his disciples, who had cautiously started to regroup as the persecution against them in Kamakura abated. With their support, his evangelical efforts were increasingly successful, and pictorial evidence of this can still be seen in some of Sado's principal temples: many contain votive paintings of him at work, preaching in the snow to groups of ragged islanders with spiky white beards, or receiving their petitions in rocky shoreside caves.

Ball of Fire

The name Tsukahara is now only in occasional use: today the village is called Niibo and a large temple called Kompon-ji now stands on the site where Nichiren was first detained. At the front is a large, carefully laid out garden that illustrates aspects of paradise, centering on a clutch of lotus flowers in the Pond of Mercy. "All about the Pond," as one account describes it, "wondrous flowers bloom, each one like a different-colored jewel. The blues and yellows sparkle, the reds and whites vibrate, and all shimmer in response to the slightest breezes. Palaces and pavilions, trees decked with blossom, trilling birds and celestial angels playing heavenly music complete the brilliant and colorful scene."

What with the numerous Ponds of Mercy, the cute little bridges and waterwheels, the variegated patches of moss, and the neatly fenced pathways, the brilliant and colorful scene was altogether too contrived for this outsider's taste. To some degree, all religious sects consist of caged people who spend a lot of time congratulating each other on the quality of the bars; but in the context of Japanese Buddhism in general, Nichiren-shu's love affair with ornamentation seems excessive to the point of perversity, in striking contrast to the cool austerity that dignifies the temples of its rivals. However, this view is not wholly just: the sect's association with wealth—but not privilege—is a direct legacy of its peculiar history. Originally favored by the poor, by Edo times it had become dominant among merchants and traders, then legally defined as the lowest of the four social classes; and when Japanese cities were ravaged by fire and earthquake, as happened all too often, it was not Pure Land ritual or Zen serenity that repaired the damage, but Nichiren-shu money. Today, awareness of the practical value of wealth persists, along with a vigorous popularity: I counted fourteen large, air-conditioned buses outside Kompon-ji, from which eager groups of smartly dressed followers with notebooks and cameras were led round the grounds by elegant young women in crisp dark blue uniforms and snow-white gloves. These guides conducted their tours at a brisk pace, stopping at all the right places to explain the architectural features and other points of

177

SADO: JAPAN'S ISLAND IN EXILE

interest described in the brochures. A complementary building of some kind was being constructed on a patch of land next door to the temple, and, although it had not yet taken shape, I felt sure that it was destined to be a Nichiren Lecture Hall, a Nichiren Training Center, or possibly even a five-star Nichiren Hotel. Lavish spending, fueled as ever by contributions from compliant devotees, proceeds side by side with the ardent evangelism that is Nichiren-shu's oldest tradition. Outsiders disapprove: such behavior is immodest, vulgar, un-Japanese. Affecting a calm indifference, the followers ignore them.

Inside the temple, the glitter had been slapped on in bucketfuls. Gleaming with gold and glowing with red lacquer, the focus was a complicated multilevel altar structure made up of boxes and shelves, drawers and lecterns, drapes and ribbons, golden flowers and golden bells. And while I was standing there looking at it, feeling faintly sick, a young monk sidled up beside me and inquired where I had come from. From Matsugasaki, I told him. I walked here over the mountains, the same way Nichiren had come. At this he took a step back, looking completely amazed.

"You walked?"

"That's right."

"From Matsugasaki?"

"Yes, from Matsugasaki."

"But how did you . . . I mean . . . you really *walked?*"

"Yes, walked. Is that so strange?"

"Oh no, by no means, not at all." But he still hadn't got it. "Didn't you come by bus?"

"No, I walked. As I just told you."

"On your own two legs?"

"Of course on my own two legs!"

"But why?"

I had had about enough of this. "Look," I said, "I've come here to see the temple. Here it is, and I've seen it. Now I'm going to have a look at the paintings. Is that all right with you?"

He nodded wordlessly. A foreigner! What could a foreign-

178

Ball of Fire

er be doing here? And walking! When he could just as easily have taken the bus! Why would he do such a thing?

The paintings were vividly colored modern reproductions of not-very-old originals, whose interest value was more in the subject than the execution. The first showed Nichiren in the boat bringing him to Sado. There was a tremendous storm in progress and everyone was praying in terror or clinging onto some part of the boat and screaming. Only Nichiren looked unmoved: he was depicted holding a pole out over the water, as if to calm the raging waves. The next showed Nichiren in the little hut at Tsukahara, kneeling down with his eyes closed and fingering his prayer beads. In the distance, wearing straw boots, blue trousers, and a yellow jacket patterned with green leaves, the kindly Abutsubo was approaching with a bag of supplies in his hand and a straw mat slung across his head and shoulders to keep off the heavily falling snow. Another picture illustrated the Great Debate: Nichiren was shown sitting on a rush mat with a pile of sutras and documents in front of him on a low table, while the priests of Sado stood around in agitated postures, waving scrolls in their hands and tugging at their wispy beards. Finally there was a painting of Nichiren in his later days on Sado: this time he was shown on a mountaintop beside a red pine, praying with his hands together while a deep red sun rose over the tops of the distant hills.

Exile on Sado, which was supposed to finish him off, turned out to be just an interlude in Nichiren's career. Most of his two and a half years there were spent amplifying his doctrine and redefining his mission as the savior of his country. Meanwhile, events in Kamakura, including further threats from Kublai Khan and bitter squabbles among the still-dominant Hojo family, had borne out many of his predictions. His stock was up, and the government felt obliged to rethink its attitude. Persistent lobbying for his release by his friends and disciples tipped the balance, and in March 1274, the regent Tokimune issued an official pardon. Soon after it reached the island, early the following month, Nichiren set sail for the mainland and returned to the capital.

179

Outside the temple, the garden was more crowded than ever, so I had a quick lunch of fried noodles at a stall in the car park and then set off to hitchhike back to Matsugasaki and resume my journey. Almost at once I got a lift from a local council worker and then another from a young man in a small bus who was driving to Chokoku-ji to pick up a group of sightseers. Traffic then dried up completely, so I unloaded my pack, took off my boots, and sat for a while cooling my feet in the clear, cold water of a rocky stream. An old woman with a net bag full of shiny black eggplants stopped to pass the time of day, and I asked her if she lived nearby. "No, no," she said, "I'm a stranger here. I don't know this area at all. I'm from Tsuka-hara." This answer seemed a little strange, since Tsukahara was only two or three miles away, but I was intrigued by her use of the old name; it was the only time I ever heard it spoken aloud.

Finally a battered old pickup swung into view and lurched to a halt in response to my waving thumb. The driver was a stout little man with a head like a watermelon and a carefully waxed mustache that looked as if he glued it into place every morning before breakfast. Beside him in the cab sat his wife, a middle-aged woman with powerful, blunt-fingered hands and brawny forearms. They were dressed for an excursion, the husband in polished black shoes, neatly creased charcoal slacks, a mustard-color sports shirt, and a gray windcheater, and the wife in those dull, opaque stockings favored by older ladies, a skirt made of something like blanket material, and a brown cardigan with the sleeves rolled up. The cab was cluttered with their belongings, so I made as if to climb up behind. But the wife wouldn't hear of it. "We'll soon clear this stuff out," she exclaimed, and began dragging bags and coats and boxes out of the cab and heaving them into the back. Standing up on the trailer, lashed in place by a web of thick ropes, was a brown fiberglass object that looked like a phone box. "It's a toilet, you see," said the wife. "We're taking it over to Niigata tonight, on the ferry. It's going to a building site. Belongs to my husband's company. Come on, in you get. I'll go in the middle." We squeezed into the little cab and bounced off up toward the

Ball of Fire

mountains. I told them I had walked this way earlier in the day, and made a few appreciative comments about the scenery, the flowers, and the birdsong. The woman was unimpressed. "We wouldn't know anything about all that," she said briskly. "We live by the sea. I was born there—never learned anything about the mountains." She spoke as if the two were mutually exclusive, like different planets. The husband said nothing, but kept turning his head toward me and staring hard, as if he couldn't understand how a foreigner had ended up in his truck. I huddled up against the door and looked out of the window, hoping he would concentrate on the driving. Either he didn't know the road or else he was new to the truck, because he kept misjudging his position and driving with the nearside wheels too close to the verge. At one point, as we plunged quickly down toward another hairpin, I knew for certain we were going to smash into a sturdy concrete telegraph pole; but at the very last second the man twitched the steering wheel and the collision was avoided. Instead there was a loud smash and the wing mirror disappeared. "You should be more careful," said the wife in a gently reproving voice. "Now we'll have to get another of those in Niigata."

They dropped me on the main road in Oda and rattled off up the coast with the toilet swaying slightly behind them. It was a brilliant day, the sun's fierce heat tempered by a steady breeze that drove armies of white-crested waves across a wide blue sea toward the shore.

At Matsugasaki I bought a can of beer and sat in the shade of an old pine to drink it, thinking over the end of the Nichiren story. His pardon arrived, he left Sado, and he traveled back to Kamakura. Sounds easy. But the journey was no cakewalk. It was April, a time of changeable weather, and the stony trails, often no more than footpaths, were soft and muddy with snowmelt. Winding along the edges of rivers, zigzagging up wind-blasted mountainsides, threading through black forests, such trails were never easy going. And this north-south route between Echigo and the Pacific was no Tokaido Road. It had no refinements, no sections decoratively lined with cherry trees, no feisty

181

inns with jolly landlords serving hearty local fare and take your pick from my stable of tasty wenches. Travelers had to be on their guard, move in groups, carry their own means of defense. And for Nichiren, there was an extra danger. His reputation preceded him. Something of his story was known everywhere, and its dissident flavor antagonized the conservative-minded provincials whose villages and fiefs he rode through. Three or four attempts were made to intercept and kill him, but these were expected; Nichiren had been provided with an escort of soldiers, ready to fight. They had to be. Every place had local toughs eager for a chance to snap at the heels of the Great Troublemaker. Everyone wanted the standing to be gained from killing the heretic.

None of them succeeded, and Nichiren arrived back in Kamakura to a tumultuous welcome from his followers. In government circles, it was hoped that two and a half years on Sado had mellowed him out—at least enough to join in the general praying for victory over the Mongols, whose threatened rerun of their recently failed invasion was awaited with dread. Ten days after his return, Nichiren was invited to the regent's residence where, to his wry amusement, his old enemy Hei no Saemon had been given the task of expressing official goodwill. After an inconclusive discussion about what would happen next, Nichiren was offered a provisional peacemaking package: money, high ecclesiastical rank, and a public grant for his preaching. He refused. Horns were locked as before. Accusations and intrigues resumed.

After only two months of it, Nichiren had had enough. He retired to a place called Minobu, on the west side of Mt. Fuji, where a wealthy follower built him a hut on a patch of level ground "the size of the palm of my hand," surrounded by high peaks. "This spot is secluded from worldly life," he noted with satisfaction. "There are no people living around here at all." There were no worldly comforts, either. In the depths of winter, the snow sometimes lay so deep that it covered the roof of his hut. "The walls are encrusted with ice and the long, dangling icicles remind me of the garlands used to decorate shrines."

Ball of Fire

Some of his supporters were disappointed by his withdrawal from the public stage, but Nichiren himself had no doubts. "I had always resolved to repeat my remonstrances three times," he wrote in explanation, "and then, if they failed, to retire." It was the only course. If he had continued as before, he would have ended up with the same result—another term of exile or, more likely, execution.

The Mongol menace remained, and in August 1281 they showed up again—this time with a massive force of 140,000 men in 4,000 ships. Despite urgent warnings from their crews, Korean levies who knew the local weather, the slow-moving Mongols were still in mid-disembarkation when they were struck by a massive typhoon. Their fleet was destroyed and the invasion abandoned. In Japan there was wild public rejoicing at the success of this "divine wind," or *kamikaze*, but the old dissident in Minobu still recognized a lucky break when he saw one. "The enemy's ships were scattered by a typhoon," he wrote, "but all you hear now is people boasting of a great victory, as if they had done it all themselves. The priests, of course, are the same as ever; they pretend that victory was the result of their prayers. But ask them whether they took the head of the Mongol king! Whatever they say, just ask them that!"

This was his last pronouncement on public events. Early the following year, his sixtieth, he began to show symptoms of a cancer in the digestive organs. "For ten days I have taken no food," he wrote. "My body feels like stone, and my chest is as cold as ice." A few months later he set out to try a hot spring cure, but died on the journey.

* * *

I drained the last of the beer and set off again up the road. A few miles beyond Matsugasaki, a construction gang had built a short strip of road down to a narrow beach from which they were now removing pebbles in dump-truck loads. This involved driving the trucks down onto the beach, filling them up, and then reversing back up the hill onto the main road. A woman in a grubby white bonnet had the job of warning oncoming

183

The gateball tournament

traffic, when there was any. She beckoned secretively to me with a black-gloved hand as I went by, so I went across to her, thinking she had something to show me. But all she wanted was a few minutes' company. "All day I'm here," she moaned, shaking her head, "all day, every day from eight in the morning until six. Nothing happens. No one to talk to. It's lonely." "Well at least it's a job," I said, trying to look on the bright side. "At least there's a payday at the end of the month." "Payday?" she spat. "A hundred thousand yen isn't a payday. Not when you've got a husband that drinks as much as mine does. And children to support. No, the pay is no good. But that's Sado," she added gloomily. "Sado isn't Tokyo. It's far away—far away from every-where. That's why there's no money here. All jobs have low pay on Sado."

One by one, the little villages drifted past—clusters of tim-ber shacks draped with morning glories and huddled together beside stony patches of beach, old women hobbling by with bas-kets of onions, mangy cats yawning in the shade of dusty yards, battered dinghies drawn up under rickety bamboo shelters, a litter of ropes, nets, floats, barrels, and planks scattered at ran-dom on the ground, and here and there a few pathetic piles of

Ball of Fire

yellowing mushrooms or silvery fish spread out on mats to dry in the sun. This was the quietest, least-visited part of Sado I had yet seen and, apart from the smooth tarmac road and the cola machines, the closest to old-time rural Japan—silent, poor, self-absorbed, and locked in unchanging monotony. Even the passage of a stranger was an Event, as likely to provoke alarm as curiosity. One old woman, who had been sitting on the seawall, languidly packing vegetables into a straw basket, suddenly caught sight of me as I rounded the corner; she sprang up in fright, dropped the basket over the wall, and skittered across to the other side of the road like a cat panicked by a dog, disappearing soundlessly into a dark and cobwebbed doorway.

Toward the end of the afternoon I arrived at a place called Noura. By this time I was about ready for an Event myself—and so infectious was the atmosphere of torpor along the Uchikaifu coast that the discovery of a gateball tournament in progress seemed like a big deal. There were about a dozen players, all women, taking it in turns to knock their wooden balls around a dusty patch of ground with cut-down croquet mallets. At some stage the balls were supposed to pass through three hoops placed around a central wooden pole, but another important feature of the game involved using one's own ball to bash those of the other players off the playing area. A wizened old woman was showing how it should be done, scampering gleefully from one spot to the next and scattering the opposition with mighty blows of her mallet, while her opponents watched from a bench, exclaiming at her prowess and wagging their heads in dismay.

Noura had a pretty arc of sandy beach, a few shops, a temple in a wooded hollow, and behind that, an inn with a carefully tended garden. I felt I had covered enough miles for one day; what I fancied was a good soak in the bath and then a couple of quiet cans of beer down on the beach. So I opened the inn door and called out for attention. After a few moments, a toothless ancient emerged, his bleary eyes indicating that I had disturbed his afternoon sleep, and shuffled forward to greet the new arrival. At the sight of a sweaty, unshaven foreigner he shiv-

SADO: JAPAN'S ISLAND IN EXILE

ered nervously, then took half a pace backward and began to rub his hands as if washing them. Most unfortunately, he explained, his inn was still closed—in fact his wife was away visiting relatives at present—but if I was looking for a place to stay, he was glad to be able to give me good news. There were inns in the next village, four of them, all already open for the season, all of the very best quality, and all thirsting for custom. "Hardly anyone stays here in Noura," he said with an apologetic chuckle. "But up the road there, that's a different matter. Coaches stop there, often—there's room for lots of people. They have parties—singing, food, everything! That's the way, down there!" He gestured encouragingly at the road outside. "How far is it?" I asked him. "A couple of kilometers?" "Oh no, nothing like as much as that," he said as he began to slide the door shut. "You'll be there in no time! Good-bye!"

Any inn may be shut at any time and for any reason, but when you're tired and hungry and your needs are modest, and you get turned down in a place that obviously needs every guest it can get, it's easy to get suspicious. Perhaps they don't like the look of you, or they think you won't be able to eat their food, or they're afraid you may make some demand that they can't fulfill. When my wife and I made our first trips to Sado, nearly twenty years before, I used to lurk down the street or hide in the bushes outside while she went in to make the arrangements for a room; if the management caught sight of a foreigner before the deal was struck, there would always be a problem. Nowadays, things were different—but I always prefaced my request for a room with a lengthy speech about where I had come from and what I was doing, just to make sure they realized that communication was possible. It didn't always work, but so what? The next place might be better, or cheaper, or friendlier, or more convenient.

In the next village there were not four inns, but two. One was boarded up. The other contained no one but a deaf old granny. "Everyone's out," she told me. "It probably wouldn't be convenient for you to stay." Obviously she would be the one to catch hell if she installed a foreigner while the owners were out.

186

Ball of Fire

But fortunately, she had good news too. There were four other inns not far away. In the next village.

There were, too. At the first three I tried, no one answered the door. Were they all telephoning ahead, warning their colleagues about a monster at large in the area? No, of course not. Don't be so paranoid. Look, there's the last one—better give it a try. As I approached the door, something squashy happened in my right boot and my sock felt wet. Must have burst a blister. I opened the door and called out "*Gomen kudasai!*"

No one answered, although I could hear voices coming from the kitchen. I called out again. Nothing happened. I tried again, louder. Still nothing. It reminded me of a story about a foreigner who was traveling in rural Japan years ago and suddenly realized he was lost. As darkness fell, he spotted a lonely farm house with a light inside and smoke coming from the chimney. Intending to ask for a night's lodging, he strode up to the house and knocked briskly on the door. There was no answer, so he knocked again . . . and again, and again. After a long interval, the door was cautiously opened and the family came out to inspect him. At first they wouldn't let him into the house—not until he had allowed the farmer to walk round behind him and check his clothes at the back. The explanation, when he eventually worked it out, was that no one ever knocks at a door in Japan; the visitor always opens it himself and then calls out to the people inside. When they heard the knocking, the family thought it was a tail tapping against their door—the tail of a ghostly, dangerous, shape-changing fox. So they weren't letting the stranger in until they had checked behind him to see if there was a tail there or not. But dammit, surely these bloody innkeepers hadn't mistaken me for a fox? I had opened the door and called out normally, hadn't I? I stood there fuming, allowing anger to boil up inside me—invariably a mistake in Japan. I knew that, but didn't care. I would damned well stand there and holler till these people came to the door, even if I had to wait for an hour. It wasn't an hour, but it felt like it. Eventually a woman came. A room? Oh how unfortunate! They were all just getting ready to go out for the evening!

187

To a relative's party in Akadomari! What a pity! Ha ha! So of course they weren't taking in any guests. Still, that's life. People make plans, things don't always fit in. But there was no need to be downhearted. It wasn't all bad news, not by any means. Because the woman knew a couple of other inns where she was sure I could get a room for the night. In fact she was certain, because she herself had met a couple of people that very day who told her they had stayed there. I held up my hand. "Don't tell me where they are—let me guess. The next village?"

By the time the next village came in sight I had been walking for more than twelve hours and could hardly manage another step. My feet felt like lumps of raw meat, and I was leaning my full weight on Snake Frightener, all snake-frightening and dog-bashing duties suspended. If I couldn't find an inn here, the hell with it. I couldn't go any further; if necessary I would scramble down to the beach and crash out on the stones.

"Hey, what's happened to you? You look exhausted!" I looked up and saw a bespectacled young man in a green track-suit leaning in the doorway of a small police box, the kind of substation often found in country areas, attached to a private home. He surveyed me with a friendly smile, a cigarette dangling from his hand. A battered red Suzuki compact stood parked on a strip of concrete beside the road.

"Ha ha! Well yes, to tell you the truth I am a little tired. You know, walking along, enjoying myself, seeing all the sights of Sado—I do believe I lost track of the time! And now it's getting toward the end of the day so I'm looking for somewhere to stay."

The policeman turned his head slightly and called over his shoulder "Oi! You!" Then he turned back to me. "Take that pack off and come inside. Sit down for a moment and have a rest. Place to stay? We'll fix you up." There was a scuttling noise from behind him and his wife appeared, wiping her hands on a cloth. "Look what we've got here," he told her. "A customer! He's walking round Sado, and now he needs a place to stay. I'm going to call Tadauchi-san. He's started taking guests, I know. I was down there this morning. Our friend here can sit down in my office for a few minutes and rest. Get some tea for him."

188

Ball of Fire

"We don't get a lot of foreigners round here, you know," he went on. "Not at this time of year, anyway. Summer's different, of course. There's quite a few then. They like to go camping. I see you've been doing some camping too."

"That's right, I have," I told him. "But today, seeing how hot it's been and everything, I'd like to get a room and a bath."

The policeman's wife came in with two cups of green tea and two rice crackers wrapped in cellophane on a small, round tray.

"Don't worry, we'll get you a room. Now where's Tadauchi's number?" He opened a drawer, flipped through a card index, and then punched a few buttons on the telephone. "Tadauchi-san? Kataoka here. Yes, and good evening to you too! Now listen—I've got a chap here in the police box who needs a room. Looks pretty tired. He's on some sort of walking tour. You can take him, can't you? You can? Good, good. Yes, I'll run him down shortly. Ten minutes? Fine. Oh and by the way—he's a foreigner. Speaks Japanese, though. Food? Don't worry about it. He's just been telling me—eats anything that's going. Thanks then—good-bye!"

He replaced the receiver, looked up at me, and grinned. "See?" he said. "That's how to do it. Get the room fixed up first and tell them you're a foreigner afterward. Otherwise . . . well, sometimes they're not sure if it will work out or not."

After we finished the tea, this most excellent and unusual policeman offered to put my gear in the back of his compact and drive me down into the village. Just as we were setting off, a pickup whizzed by, missing the front of the Suzuki by inches, and careered down the hill and along the edge of the bay. "That Hanamura," said the policeman with a sigh. "I'll have to have a word with him again. The way he drives, he's just bound to have an accident sometime. But I suppose he's in a hurry—he's running a bit late for the ferry. They're going over to Niigata tonight, him and his wife." But I knew that already. As the pickup roared across the bay and disappeared up the hill on the other side, I could still see the brown fiberglass toilet firmly roped in place on the back.

189

DAY 8

RAFTS WHERE SEAGULLS CROWD

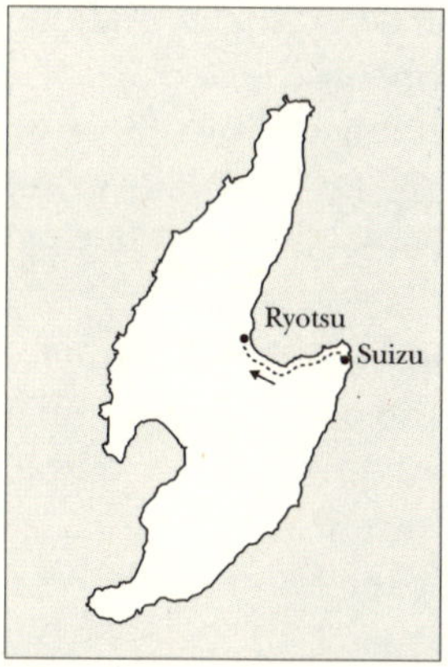

There must have been a road somewhere round the back, but the policeman left his car on the main street of the village and led me to the front of the inn down a maze of narrow, stone-flagged alleyways where morning glories grew on flimsy wooden trellises and bushy hydrangeas sprouted in tiny, carefully tended gardens. Thanks to my official escort, the Tadauchis' welcome could hardly have been warmer; setting me up with a first-floor room that overlooked a sea of uneven, gray-tiled roofs, the husband bustled off to fetch cold beer while his wife, grinning broadly to reveal a phalanx of steel teeth, insisted on collecting all my dirty clothes in a basket and carrying them away to the washing machine.

There was a TV set on the landing outside the room, and I slumped in a chair in front of it to drink the beer and watch the weather forecast. Just as it was coming on, there were footfalls on the stairs, and I was joined by a young couple who were also guests at the inn. The man had been to university in Canada and

190

Rafts Where Seagulls Crowd

was delighted to find a foreigner with whom to resurrect his fragmented English. He worked for a trading company in Tokyo, he explained; some relative of his fiancee had died in Niigata so they had come up for the funeral and decided to stay on for a couple of days and visit Sado. They had arrived the day before and loathed it already. The food was too rustic, the hotels too small, the towns too dull, and the bus service too slow. This last complaint may have been true, especially for getting as far off the standard tourist circuit as they now were; I asked why they hadn't chosen to stay somewhere more convenient. "Recommendation, man," said the man with a sigh. "A friend recommended this place. What a dump. There's nothing here! Makes me wish I was back in Toronto—what a place that was! Ice cream, fries, burgers as big as *this!*" He rambled on in this vein for a few minutes, lying like a cheap clock about his wonderful experiences in Canada. "Never mind," he said at last. "This is our last evening." He jerked a thumb at the girlfriend. "She's got to get back to work. Night shift. So we're getting out of here tomorrow. Goddamn time too. I won't be coming back to this place, I can tell you." He stood up. "Well, better get ready for dinner. Then we'll get together. Have a few drinks. Talk some English. I like talking English. Whaddya say, hey?" He patted me on the shoulder, picked up their bags, and disappeared up the corridor. ". . . and that's all for now," said a voice from the TV. "The next weather forecast will be after the ten o'clock news."

After dinner, pleading exhaustion, I retired to my room and fell into bed. But I couldn't go to sleep. There was a strange noise somewhere in the inn—an insistent noise, maddeningly repetitive, familiar yet at the same time unfamiliar, because rarely heard in Japan. It was two young boys, aged about seven, arguing with each other in terrible whining tones—not just the usual short spat, but on and on, repeating the same slow, whining cadence, up and down, again and again. There was no making out the words, but the tones were clear enough: "Give that back, it belongs to *me!*" "No it doesn't, it belongs to *me!*" "It's *mine*—give it *back!*" "I'm not *going* to. It belongs to *me!*" I had half a mind to go and find them, give

191

SADO: JAPAN'S ISLAND IN EXILE

them each a good clout, but I was too tired to move. And eventually, when the noise refused to stop, when it had gone on even longer than the stubborn obstinacy of young boys could maintain, it dawned on me that it wasn't being made by children at all, nor even by two voices but only by one—an adult voice, it now seemed, a retarded aunt perhaps, shut away alone in some other part of the inn like Mrs. Rochester and abandoned to her compulsive, interminable groaning. No one interfered or sought to soothe her. Why should they? They heard it every day, they were used to it. They probably didn't even notice any more. Groaning? Oh, *that* groaning.

Brilliant sunshine streaming through the window early the next morning filled in the blank left by the missed weather forecast, and when I came downstairs all packed up and ready to go I found Mrs. Tadauchi waiting for me by the front door with my clean laundry. She hadn't had time to iron it yet, she told me apologetically, but would get it done while I was eating breakfast. I didn't feel much like eating, but Mrs. Tadauchi expressed such alarm at the thought of anyone starting the day without food that I felt obliged to change my mind. So I sat alone in the dining room, wading through fish, rice, pickles, and seaweed soup while she bustled back and forth with the dishes and made approving noises, pausing occasionally to give a good cackle that showed off her remarkable steel teeth. She particularly wanted to know why I was walking round Sado, and seemed disappointed to learn that the motive was pleasure. "So it's just a holiday, then?" she asked. Typical of a foreigner! Foreigners are forever taking holidays. Not like the Japanese. The Japanese are a race of real workers. At it every day, from early to late. Except on Sundays, when they sprawl in front of the TV and get drunk. But Sunday isn't a holiday—just a day off work. Mrs. Tadauchi would have been more satisfied if I had been studying Sado dialects for my postgraduate thesis, or comparing rock formations, or measuring tides, or collecting seashells. Anything with a proper purpose would have been all right—even undertaking a pilgrimage. But I wasn't going through the pilgrimage conversation again. That joke was wear-

Rafts Where Seagulls Crowd

ing thin. Although, as a matter of fact, the journey round Sado *was* feeling more and more like a pilgrimage every day. Especially now, with only a dozen or so miles left to complete the full circle. Even if I dawdled, as I firmly intended, I would be back in Ryotsu by lunchtime.

Beyond the narrow little alleys and across the main road, the harbor scene was bathed in golden light. The water shimmered with it, huge opalescent patches of sparkling yellow and peachy pink that slowly undulated on the swell, then broke into jagged dancing fragments as the boats cut through them on their way to the open sea. Even the walls of the Fisherman's Cooperative shed a warm glow, burnt orange and dusty ochre scarred by streaks of rusty, chili-pepper red where the concrete had cracked and crumbled, exposing the steel rods inside to the corroding salt air. Beside the ragged line of pickups that brought the fishermen to work lay a pile of nets, a few coils of gray, fraying rope, and a jumbled heap of sea-blackened octopus pots. Somewhere out of sight an engine fired, and then a man in green overalls drove round the corner in a battered forklift truck and stopped in front of a tall stack of empty fish crates. Guided by levers, the forks rose up their shafts with a soft mechanical hum, picked a dozen crates off the top of the stack, and deposited them on the ground with a dry clatter. The sound disturbed a group of kites watching from the telegraph wire overhead; they shifted uneasily, half-opened their wings, and then hunched down again, their eyes toward the sea, patiently waiting for the fishing boats' return.

The road climbed out of town up a tree-shaded gully, then swung inland and headed north with fields of young green rice on either side. An easy hour's walking brought me within sight of the last of the four great points of Sado. The first was Futatsugame, the islet at the northern tip; the second was the end of Nanaura Kaigan, at the northern extremity of long, sweeping Mano Bay; the third was Sawasaki in the far southwest, close to the enclave of the demon drummers; and this last was Himezaki, whose lighthouse marks the way for the ferries and fishing boats in and out of Ryotsu Bay.

SADO: JAPAN'S ISLAND IN EXILE

To reach the lighthouse I had to turn off the main road and follow a twisting, dun-colored track that wound down the cliff through dark pine woods. At the bottom of the hill it met a footpath that ran along the back of a stony beach and linked up with a system of sea-splashed bridges and walkways leading around the very tip of the point. Along the way it passed through a deserted cove with boats drawn up above the tide line and a pretty little shrine at the far end. The shrine doors were open, and on the shelf stood a dirty glass vase with a few dead flowers hanging limply over the rim. These I replaced with a bunch of scruffy buttercups, filling the vase with fresh water from a stream that trickled out onto the shingle nearby. Then I stepped back, bowed, and said a short prayer for the safety and well-being of travelers and good catches for the fishermen whose boats were drawn up behind me. Apart from routine mumblings of Church liturgy, praying aloud is rather against an Englishman's instincts—not the sort of thing one would, er, care to be seen doing, especially out in the open, on a beach, while bowing down to a graven idol. But after a week of doing it several times a day, I no longer found it strange. Quite the opposite: it felt good, refreshing even, just putting the hands together, bowing to the shrine, making requests and expressing thanks in an ordinary tone of voice. Some people, it's true, prefer the built-in gravitas of church surroundings, the reverential hush, the candles, the drapes, the choir stalls, the statues, the pictures, and the stained glass. These things work to concentrate the mind, confer solemnity, sharpen the focus on humility and truth. Japan's roadside shrines offer something quite different—something light, friendly, accessible, perfectly in tune with the ebb and flow of unchanging daily life.

I clambered round the rocks at the end of the point and followed the path up onto the top of the headland. The view was stunning: a backdrop of steep mountains, the houses and wharves of Ryotsu spread out along the distant shore, fierce sunlight glinting off the sea, and the day's first ferry to Niigata, lightly loaded and high in the water, steaming past the harbor wall and out into the bay. All around where I stood the land was divid-

194

Rafts Where Seagulls Crowd

ed into the usual patchwork of paddies, and a short way ahead I could see a young woman struggling along with a wheelbarrow on which was balanced a large blue plastic tub of liquid fertilizer. As I watched, she turned off the path to cross a little plank bridge over a stream; but the wheel slipped off the plank and jammed in the ditch between the narrow banks. I went across and helped her haul it out again, watched in silence by a tiny baby who was strapped to her back in a quilted sling. When mothers on Sado have work to do, they go and do it; if there's no one at home to look after the baby, then hup! the baby goes up on their back and comes along too. Out in the open all day, the infants start learning about their surroundings right away—the shapes of trees and rocks, the colors of things that grow, the sounds of the sea, the feel of the wind, the songs and movements of people sharing work in the fields. All other things being equal, it's no wonder that many of them still grow up to be simple and happy, rooted in a real life that they fully understand.

On the outskirts of Nojo was a white-painted primary school surrounded by a high wall, but not high enough to conceal from the children that something weird was about to pass by. As I came clunking down the road, a line of grinning faces popped up along the top of the wall like so many Humpty Dumpties, giggling and calling out "America! Hey you, America! Good morning!" Immediately, from somewhere behind them, a teacher growled, and they all disappeared together, shrieking with excitement.

Opposite the school, a concrete jetty with a dozen small boats moored to it extended out into the sea like a fat finger. It pointed toward an islet that was linked to the end of the jetty by an old-fashioned curved bridge painted a bright vermilion. A few stunted pines grew where their roots could find purchase in the stony soil, and a white-painted shrine, this one with the doors firmly shut, huddled as if for shelter in the lee of a large, badly fractured rock.

At the far end of the islet, the sea was heaving gently, sloshing in and out of deep pools almost completely encircled by rocks. Here I came upon an old man in long green waders

195

"The two of us"

who was gravely raking seaweed from the water and loading it into a large plastic laundry basket. The fleshy stem of each plant was rooted in the seabed, from where it grew upward in long, thin strands. Bracing himself in position on the rocks, the man took up a bamboo pole about ten feet long, with a rusty little sickle on the end, guided it down through the water, and made a quick cut through the base of as many plants as he could reach from where he was standing. In a few minutes the surface was covered with strands of weed, which floated there like huge tresses of hair. These he hauled shoreward with the sickle, switching at the last moment to a sturdy short-handled rake more suited to lifting them out of the water. It was a little living, he explained, to supplement his pension. Every morning he scoured the coast for this weed, which was called *tsurumo,* and in the afternoon he pushed it round on a handcart and sold it to anyone who would buy. Preparation was easy: the *tsurumo* was cut into bite-size pieces, bruised in a mortar for tenderness, then boiled and eaten in soup.

Although it was still early the sun was already blazing—surely the hottest day since I had set out—so at the next opportunity I turned off the road on a track that led down to a beach, flung my clothes on the sand, and ran into the water. It felt good, but the cold made me gasp like a punch in the stomach; after a few minutes I scrambled out again and sat on the ground to dry off. And while I was there I heard the sound of an engine and looked up to see a car bumping down the same track to the beach.

Rafts Where Seagulls Crowd

Actually it wasn't a car but a Mitsubishi Pajero, one of those four-wheel-drive, all-terrain vehicles favored by the rugged adventurer brigade. This one looked brand new: in the driving seat, hunched over the wheel in a purposeful attitude, sat a thin-faced man in a yellow baseball cap, chewing gum. Beside him was his wife, in a floppy, wide-brimmed hat that failed to hide the nervous look on her face. Two young children were standing up on the back seat, their faces glued to the windows and their mouths open in expectation. It was obviously family test drive time.

First the man roared down the full length of the beach and made a sweeping turn at the far end. Spraying sand to left and right, the huge tires gouged deep tracks and passed across a patch of morning glories, mangling the pale pink flowers to pulp. Excellent. The man enjoyed that. The children too. Their mouths were open, wider than ever—they were screaming with excitement. So the man revved up the engine and did it again. The third run was the best yet: this time, the machine bounced across its own tracks, bucking like a donkey. The beach looked as though it had been under heavy mortar fire for hours. As for the morning glories, they had disappeared. Wonderful! The test drive was going well. Pajeros cost a lot of money, but were clearly worth every penny.

Now the man looked around for a fresh challenge. At one end of the beach was a wide area of rock littered with loose boulders and scooped out here and there by rock pools that contained delicate water plants, red and yellow anemones, crabs, and tiny fish, all waiting together for the returning tide. This looked ideal. The Pajero bumped up onto the rocks as eagerly as a dog bounding up a staircase. A couple of good-size boulders bounced off the bull bars in front with a clang. Fractured shards of rock squirted out from under the tires and pinged off their neighbors or sailed skyward before stabbing soundlessly into the churned-up sand. One wheel smashed through a rockpool in a cloud of spray, thrillingly fast but just too fast for me to spot any broken claws, legs, or other bits of crab spinning through the air. And then, just when it seemed

197

that there was nothing left to wreck, fate came up with one last suggestion.

Having brought the Pajero to a sudden, shuddering stop, the man leaned out of the window, chewing fiercely on his gum, and glanced casually back over his shoulder. He was feeling tough as hell and looked it—like Marlboro Man with a fresh pack of smokes in his jeans and a pint of good ol' rye whisky in his gut. Slamming into reverse, he gave the steering wheel a good twist, kicked on the throttle, and lurched backward a few yards, banging two pumpkin-size rocks out of his way as easily as if they were tennis balls. But behind them, unfortunately, was a much deeper pool than any he had sampled so far, and his offside rear wheel now dropped straight into it with a sickening metallic crunch. The Pajero sat there at a drunken angle, apparently resting on its springs. Even the adjacent door sill, I noted with pleasure, had a bad dent underneath.

At first, the man tried to look on the bright side. This was the kind of thing the four-wheel-driver had to expect. Mitsubishi's engineers certainly expected it—that was why they had made the Pajero as tough as a tank. Didn't it say so in the brochure—on page 4, beside that picture of the All-Terrain Wizard battling up a rock-strewn mountain slope at forty-five degrees? He settled into position, slipped the gear back into first, and tried to move forward. The machine strained a bit, but didn't budge. He tried again, revving harder. Nothing. Then a third time. The engine screamed, smoke blasted from the exhaust pipe, but the Pajero stayed where it was, stuck fast. Of course, it would come out eventually. But it looked like a tractor job to me.

For a brief moment there was silence. Then the doors opened, and the family stepped gingerly out to study the situation. Daddy didn't need to be told that it was serious. All the toughness had gone out of him in a rush, like steam out of a fractured pipe. He sidled cautiously toward the problem, like the office weed presenting himself for a bawling out from the section chief. There was a short conference with his wife. She was holding the children's hands, one on each side, and shak-

Rafts Where Seagulls Crowd

ing her head in a censorious manner. The man hung his head, listened, and nodded. Then he stumped off up to the road to get help.

Seeing that the drama was over, I decided to get dressed and carry on to Ryotsu. I wouldn't take the road; the path looked more inviting, at least to begin with, as it continued along to the end of the beach and rounded the point. I put on my clothes, heaved on the pack, and was just about to set off when I noticed the Pajero driver's wife down on her haunches, looking intently at the front wheels. They were turned at a sharp angle, so she climbed up into the driving seat, twisted the steering wheel a couple of times, and straightened them. Then she started the engine, leaned on the accelerator, and let out the clutch. With a tremendous effort the Pajero heaved itself upward, paused for an agonizing moment on the edge of the hole, and then rolled forward to safety. The woman got out and looked at it with satisfaction. The children ran to her, laughing with pleasure. How happy they were! And what a nice surprise it would make for Daddy when he came back with the tractor!

From the point at the end of the beach I could see all the way round the bay to Ryotsu. The path meandered along the shore, skirting little coves divided from each other by low, rock-strewn headlands and passing through semiderelict hamlets with a few battered boats drawn up at the tide line. Most of the larger buildings, store sheds and boatbuilding premises, were falling to bits where they stood, their doorways choked with wild flowers, their windows smashed, and their roofs festooned with moss, ivy, and tufts of yellow grass. Despite this dereliction there were a few signs of occupation—crinkled ribbons of greeny black seaweed strung on ropes between gray, sea-bleached poles, and neatly piled stacks of firewood tied in bundles with rusty wire—but the villagers themselves must all have been out in the fields. The only ones I met were a small boy contemplating the loss of his kite, which had got badly tangled in a pair of telegraph lines, and an old woman filling a twenty-kilo plastic rice sack with coarse, gritty sand from the beach. She was planning to repair a pathway beside her house, she told me. A

SADO: JAPAN'S ISLAND IN EXILE

neighbor had given her half a bag of cement and now she was collecting the sand. What would she want with clean building sand when there was plenty of sand right here, to be had for nothing?

There had been an earthquake here a few days ago, the old woman told me, and the local temple had been damaged. I remarked that it must have been a very small one, as I hadn't been aware of it, but she gestured toward the temple with her trowel and told me to go and take a look for myself. Apart from being overgrown with buttercups and nettles the front looked normal enough, but there was another access path at the back that passed along the base of a deep gully and was now blocked with heaps of rocks and clay, the debris of a considerable land- slide. Two pairs of *torii* gates had been knocked over and the path was impassable. It certainly looked recent: the leaves on the fallen trees and plants were wilting, but still green. There was a week's work for three or four men to put things right, but no start had been made because everyone was busy with the rice planting.

Eventually the path along the beach turned aside through a copse of firs and rejoined the coast road. As I walked the last couple of miles into Ryotsu, the town came out to meet me: a couple of supermarkets, a gas station, a school, a truck depot, an advance party of new buildings straggling along the shoreward side of the road, extending the town's boundaries and marking out the area where tomorrow's more serious urban develop- ment would follow. The old village communities watched help- lessly as progress encroached on their territory. Outside a tumbledown cottage, two old men were sitting together on fish crates, drinking beer: when they called me over, I went to join them. It was a bit early in the morning to start drinking, but it reminded me of other early mornings with my father-in-law, who also believed that beer for breakfast was the right way to fight off a hangover. The old men wanted to know where I had walked from, and when I named the place, barely twelve miles away, they expressed astonishment and disbelief. Like the coming of the supermarkets, things were changing, changing so fast that for

Rafts Where Seagulls Crowd

*Offshore islet
near Suizu*

even the oldest generation the idea that anyone would cover that distance on foot when they didn't have to was almost incomprehensible. What used to be ordinary, unremarkable, the stuff of daily life, was now draining out of the common memory like water from a leaky bucket.

While we sat there, a truck pulled out of its depot opposite, signaling to turn right onto the main road. He ought to have checked to see if any other traffic was coming, but his attention was distracted by the sight of something unexpected—a foreigner!—and he pulled out without looking to left or right. Of course there had to be another truck coming, and of course they managed to avoid each other, but it reminded me again that even today, whether driving, walking, or just sitting still, a foreigner in rural Japan is always a potential traffic hazard.

On the outskirts of town, I turned away from the sea and followed a dusty track down to the edge of Lake Kamo. It was a bright, sunny noon with a light wind and just a few wisps of cloud scudding across the sky above the rocky peak of Kimpoku-san, the mountain that towered over the far side of the lake. There were gulls everywhere, some hanging almost still in the air, slowly beating their wings against the wind, some bob-

201

SADO: JAPAN'S ISLAND IN EXILE

bing on the ruffled surface of the water, and others crowded together on the oyster rafts. A good half of the lake, it seemed, was given over to oyster farming. The rafts were double-bed-size contraptions of bamboo poles tied together in rectangular frames, anchored to the bottom to stop them drifting and kept afloat by heavy glass globes lashed to the underside of the cross-pieces. A dozen or more thick ropes hung vertically down below each raft, with oysters growing on them in clusters; dividers were attached to keep about six inches of clear rope between each cluster, and there would be six or more clusters per rope depending on the depth of the water beneath. From time to time the farmers came chugging out in little boats to inspect the oysters' progress and perhaps gather in a load; day after day, the gulls came to do their own fishing or just stand on the rafts and wait for something to happen.

Beside the lake was a square building of cracked concrete that belonged to an old acquaintance of mine called Fukuda. Tall and heavily built even as a boy, Fukuda had been picked out by a visiting talent scout and sent to Tokyo at the age of thir-teen to join a sumo wrestling stable. For five years he endured the ferocious discipline but by that time it had become clear that his ability wasn't up to the demands of a professional career; so he had come home again to Sado and set up as a boatbuilder. Things went well, and he had made other invest-ments—a couple of bars, a vegetable shop in Aikawa, and this building beside the lake. At first he used it for storage, but later, after opening a new, larger boatyard on the other side of town, he kept just the ground floor for storage and converted the two floors above into apartments. One was for his own use, a place to retreat from his family and relax with friends. The other was sometimes occupied, sometimes not. Fukuda liked to keep it handy, rent it out on short lets to help someone in a jam, or lend it to old friends who came to visit him on the island.

I found Fukuda inside the storage shed having a spat with a young assistant. The bench between them was littered with tools—curved and straight planes, drill bits, wedges, pliers, and three or four traditional saws, the double-edged kind that cut on

Rafts Where Seagulls Crowd

the upstroke. Fukuda was annoyed because the lad had wasted a valuable length of timber by cutting it too short. The mistake had been made because he had been calculating in centimeters instead of the traditional unit of measurement, the *ken*. Japan went metric way back in 1885, but the old system of weights and measures refused to die—even after 1959, when the government tried to stamp it out by prohibiting the manufacture and sale of the necessary tools. This was bad enough for ordinary carpenters, but crippling for the craftsmen who specialized in rebuilding dilapidated shrines and temples. The components of such structures were always sized in multiples of the old units; if the job was done in centimeters, something would always come out wrong. Twenty years later the obstructive law was repealed, but in the meantime the carpenters had been forced to struggle on with their old units inconveniently and inaccurately expressed in centimeters: one *ken* was 182 centimeters, one *shaku* (a sixth of a *ken*) was 30.3 centimeters, and one *sun* (a tenth of a *shaku*) was . . . well, whatever it was, the metric system was a damned nuisance, that's what Fukuda thought. The new generation of apprentices would just have to sideline what they learned in school and relearn the old ways. "Use this next time!" he said fiercely, brandishing a long wooden *shaku* ruler at his assistant. "We're building boats here, not lunch boxes!"

Fukuda had to deliver some boat registration papers in town, so we went into Ryotsu together. I waited for him in the car, parked outside the municipal offices in a wide, graveled forecourt under a huge old cedar surrounded by protective railings. Then we drove along the arcaded main street and out beyond the town on the other side, turning away from the sea up a green valley that led into the mountains. Along the way we passed a huge quarrying operation: a whole mountainside had been literally torn away, stripped of its topsoil so that it looked like a huge, half-skinned carcass. The rock beneath was blasted loose, shuttled down the hill on a system of covered conveyors and sorted into enormous piles of stone and gravel, graded by size and quality. A procession of heavily laden dump trucks passed us on the narrow road, bearing this valuable cargo to

SADO: JAPAN'S ISLAND IN EXILE

construction sites all around the island. I remarked that it was sad to see a mountain torn open like that, its insides so ruthlessly plundered, but Fukuda just laughed. "I know the man who owns that quarry," he said. "He's called Mimura. We were at school together. In those days, there was nothing up here. At weekends, a group of us would get together and walk over these mountains to the other side, camp on the beach there, and then walk back again the next day. We knew all the birds then, and most of the plants too. There was always something to collect and bring home—mushrooms, berries, *warabi* shoots. Then I went away to Tokyo, and by the time I came back, Mimura's family had started this quarry. It was just a small-time operation then. But now that there's money around, construction grants from the prefectural government, it's gone crazy. People tease Mimura about it—they call him "The Man Who Sells the Earth." He doesn't like that much, but he doesn't stop either. You can't blame him. It's a good business. And it's necessary too. Sado needs to be improved. Why, even when I was a child there were villages here that could only be reached by boat. No roads at all in some places."

The mountain road climbed up in a succession of steep hairpins, some so tight that they had to be taken in first gear. Eventually, close to the top of the pass, we stopped at a white-painted hotel called the Osado Lodge and ordered a lunch of grilled fish, rice, and beer on the outdoor terrace. The hillside around us was clothed with bare turf and tangled scrub— juniper, thorn trees, and bushes of wild azalea with deep peach-pink flowers. From the terrace we could look down on the whole of the Kuninaka plain, still mostly in paddy with long, straight, water-filled ditches and clusters of shabby farm buildings, but punctuated now with modern buildings as well, auto franchises, out-of-town DIY stores, supermarkets, fast food concessions, and tracts of new, identical concrete houses. I told Fukuda my theory that Sado would always escape the worst excesses of development because of its short summer and fearsome winter, but he was unimpressed. In his opinion no building program, present or future, could be held responsible for

204

Rafts Where Seagulls Crowd

"spoiling" the island. Such changes were inevitable, and very much to be welcomed. Likewise the tourist trade: already there were something like a million visitors a year, and no good reason why that number should not go on increasing. Their money created jobs, sustained inns and hotels, even revitalized old industries like pottery and local sake-brewing. Quick, easy connections with the mainland secured reliable markets for Sado's produce—fish, rice, vegetables, and now building materials too. Islanders could come and go at will, even commute to work on the mainland if they wanted to. At last they belonged to modern Japan, were linked for the first time to everything that was going on, no longer left to rot in poverty. If that was what I meant by "spoiling" Sado, I ought to stop worrying. Sado was "spoiled" already—vitiated by modern drugs like cars, fashion, and pop music or, as Fukuda preferred to think of it, rescued at last from oblivion by the nation's newly discovered genius for creating wealth and technology. In any case, what I feared was "lost" was not lost but transformed. Some aspects declined, others prospered. All that was happening was change, and every islander with any sense was glad to see it. The clock could never be turned back, but no one who remembered the old days would want it turned back. It was all very well for me, Fukuda said, coming to Sado as a visitor. To be foreign, tied to nothing—that was easy. Living here permanently was something else. And change in Japan, he reminded me, should never be thought of as permanent. Things could fall apart any time—an economic collapse, a big earthquake, even another war. People said that was impossible, but nothing was impossible. Right now, the name of the game was prosperity, development, improvement. Tomorrow might be different. As far as he was concerned, Sado should cash in now, get all the harbors and roads that were going. Then, whatever happened in the future, nothing could take them away again.

The sound of a ship's horn blasted up to us from Ryotsu harbor where the afternoon ferry had just come in to dock. In a couple of hours she would be pulling out again and returning to Niigata. It was time to go.

205

SADO: JAPAN'S ISLAND IN EXILE

We drove back down the mountain, past the quarry, and out of the green valley to the coast. I looked across toward the mainland but as usual there was nothing to be seen. The horizon faded imperceptibly into a misty haze. It occurred to me then for the first time that Sado, singled out so long ago as a place of exile, had always been exiled itself from the rest of Japan, exiled by natural circumstances that made it seem farther and more remote than it really was. Out of sight, out of contact. In truth, Sado is not really far—only forty miles offshore—just as Japan is not really far from the mainland of Asia; but history and geography have combined in both cases to create the impression of isolation, an impression entrenched over centuries in the national psyche. Now, it would appear, things are changing. The future is knocking at Sado's door, bearing bouquets of long-awaited improvements, and Sado, impatient to end its long seclusion, reaches eagerly out to receive them. This is the only way exile ever ends in Japan, by intervention from the mainland. Already the new prosperity has seeded Sado's revival, brought hope for a more rewarding, comfortable life. But like other agents of growth, prosperity needs time to establish strong roots. For now, the island's sense of remoteness still lies deep, guarding the old ways. It won't be dissipated any time soon.

Before taking me to the ferry terminal, Fukuda had to make another quick trip in the opposite direction, to deliver a progress report to one of his customers. I asked him to drop me off at the beach where I had camped the first night, and then pick me up again on his way back into town.

After he drove away I clambered down the clover-covered embankment, picked my way across the stones, and stood by the edge of the flat gray water. Apart from the slow, rhythmic "plish" made by tiny waves breaking on the shingle, there was no sound at all. I laid Snake Frightener down at the tide line, somewhere close to where I had first found it, and then walked slowly back up to wait beside the road.

BIBLIOGRAPHY

A brief summary of Sado's tourist highlights can be found in most current guidebooks on Japan, but no comprehensive account of its history and culture has been published in English. I have gleaned useful information and insights from the following works:

Anesaki, Masaharu. *Nichiren, the Buddhist Prophet.* Harvard University Press, 1916.

Blacker, Carmen. *The Catalpa Bow: A Study of Shamanistic Practices in Japan.* George Allen and Unwin, 1975.

Brinkley, F. *A History of the Japanese People from the Earliest times to the End of the Meiji Era.* Encyclopedia Britannica, 1915.

de Visser, M. W. *The Fox and Badger in Japanese Superstition.* Transactions of the Asiatic Society of Japan, vol. 36, 1908.

————. *The Tengu.* Transactions of the Asiatic Society of Japan, vol. 36, 1908.

Fermor, Patrick Leigh. *Mani: Travels in the Southern Peloponnese.* Harper, 1958.

Gill, Tom. "Thunder Down the Coastline." *Wingspan,* 1990.

Grant, Robert Y. *Gold and Silver in Japan.* Report #128. U.S. Army GHQ Natural Resources Section, 1950.

Hall, Robert Burnett. *Sado Island.* Papers of the Michigan Academy of Science. Arts and Letters, vol. 16, 1931.

Important Trees of Japan. Report No. 119. U.S. Army GHQ Natural Resources Section, 1949.

Kaempfer, Engelbert. *The History of Japan.* Tokyo: Yushodo Booksellers, 1979.

Major Writings of Nichiren Daishonin. Nichiren Shoshu International Center, 1979.

Phelan, Nancy. *Pillow of Grass.* MacMillan, 1969.

Piggott, Juliet. *Japanese Mythology.* Hamlyn, 1969.

Rodd, Laurel Rasplica, ed. *Nichiren: Selected Writings.* University of Hawaii Press, 1980.

Stejneger. L. *Herpetology in Japan.* Smithsonian Institution, 1907.

Stierlin, Henri, ed. *Architecture of the World: Japan.* Benedikt Taschen Verlag GmbH.

Suzuki, D. T. *Zen and Japanese Culture.* Pantheon, 1959.

Waley, Arthur. *The No Plays of Japan.* George Allen and Unwin, 1921.

Yamamoto, Shunosuke. *Sado no Mujina no Hanashi.* Sado Kyodo Bunka no Kai, 1988.

Yanagita, Kunio. *Japanese Folk Tales.* Kadokawa, 1960.